AF465957

GARFIELD Classics

Volume Three

JIM DAVIS

RR

This edition first published by
Ravette Publishing 1999
Reprinted 2000, 2001, 2003, 2005, 2009

Printed and bound in Great Britain
for Ravette Publishing Limited,
PO Box 876
Horsham
West Sussex RH12 9GH

ISBN: 978-1-85304-996-5

Garfield
Who's Talking?

GARFIELD, I THINK IT'S TIME WE GROW UP, BE MORE RESPONSIBLE, TAKE A MORE MATURE OUTLOOK ON LIFE...
HEE HEE

I DON'T THINK YOU'RE TAKING ME SERIOUSLY!
I'M SORRY
JIM DAVIS

4-12
I DON'T KNOW WHAT CAME OVER ME

DON'T EAT ME. YOU'RE TOO FAT ALREADY!
GARFIELD
JIM DAVIS
1-9

WHO ARE YOU?
THIS IS YOUR CONSCIENCE SPEAKING
GARFIELD

I DON'T HAVE A CONSCIENCE
I KNOW. I'M FREE-LANCING
GARFIELD
© 1984 United Feature Syndicate,Inc.

IF YOU ARE MY CONSCIENCE, WHAT ARE YOU DOING IN MY FOOD BOWL?
I TOOK ON A FORM YOU WOULD UNDERSTAND
GARFIELD
JIM DAVIS
1-10

WHAT DO YOU REALLY LOOK LIKE?
WELL, IF YOU MUST KNOW...
GARFIELD

I LOOK LIKE EVERYONE'S MOTHER
NATCH
GARFIELD
© 1984 United Feature Syndicate, Inc.

TELL ME, CONSCIENCE, JUST WHAT DOES A CONSCIENCE DO?
GARFIELD
JIM DAVIS
1-11

IT IS MY DUTY TO MAKE YOU FEEL BAD ABOUT THINGS THAT MAKE YOU FEEL GOOD
GARFIELD

THAT'S SAD
IT'S A LIVING
GARFIELD
© 1984 United Feature Syndicate, Inc.

WELL, CONSCIENCE, IF YOU DON'T MIND, I'LL GO TO BED NOW
TAH TAH
GARFIELD
JIM DAVIS
1-12

LOOK BOTH WAYS BEFORE CROSSING THE STREET
GARFIELD

WHAT'S THAT SUPPOSED TO MEAN?
SORRY, IT WAS JUST A KNEE-JERK NAG
GARFIELD
© 1984 United Feature Syndicate, Inc.

I CAN'T BELIEVE MY CONSCIENCE IS FOLLOWING ME AROUND. I MUST BE CRACKING UP
JIM DAVIS
1-13

A LITTLE NAP-NAP SHOULD CLEAR MY HEAD

YOU SLEEP TOO MUCH
ACK

DON'T YOU THINK YOU SHOULD BE GETTING UP NOW?
JIM DAVIS
1-14

LOOK, CONSCIENCE, GET OUT OF MY LIFE. I HAVE NO USE FOR YOU
CAREFUL, FELLA, OR I'LL CALL IN MY BIG BROTHER

WHO'S HE?
GUILT
ON THE JOGGING TRACK IN 5 MINUTES, SUCKER! BE THERE!
GARFIELD

WOULDN'T IT BE GREAT IF EVERYTHING COULD TALK?

I'D GET OUT OF BED AND THE WALL WOULD SAY, "GOOD MORNING, JON." AND THE SINK WOULD SAY, "GOOD MORNING, JON."
THAT WOULDN'T BE SO HOT
© 1984 United Feature Syndicate,Inc.

JIM DAVIS 2-15
EVERY TIME A LIGHT BULB BURNED OUT, IT WOULD BE LIKE A DEATH IN THE FAMILY

GO OUTSIDE AND PLAY, GARFIELD
1-6-84
JIM DAVIS

HAVE A GOOD TIME

© 1983 United Feature Syndicate, Inc.
"HAVE A GOOD TIME," HE SAYS

JIM DAVIS

HEY, GARFIELD, DON'T EAT THE LASAGNA YET...

1-7-84

IT'S STILL TOO HOT
YOU'RE TELLING ME?!

HOW WOULD YOU LIKE YOUR
BACON PREPARED, GARFIELD?
LET'S SHOOT FOR
RECOGNIZABLE

JIM DAVIS 6-14
JON IS A
TERRIBLE
COOK. HE
COULD RUIN
CEREAL
© 195 Jnited Feature Syndicate,Inc.

BACON
FLAMBÉ,
YUM YUM

AN INTERESTING THING ABOUT FOOD...
JIM DAVIS 6-15
SUDS

ONE MINUTE IT MAY BE HAUTE CUISINE
SUDS

BUT THE INSTANT YOU PUT IT IN THE SINK, IT BECOMES GARBAGE
SUDS

HERE'S YOUR CEREAL, GARFIELD
6-16
JIM DAVIS

WHAT'S THE MATTER? AREN'T YOU HUNGRY?
NOT REALLY

I THINK ONE OF THE FLAKES JUST MOVED

JIM DAVIS 6-13
CRACK

OH, YUK!

IT'S NOT OFTEN YOU SEE A YOLK WITH A BEAK

POOKY LOVES ME.
I CAN TELL
7-3
JIM DAVIS

HE DOESN'T TALK, HE DOESN'T
WALK, HE DOESN'T THINK

A LITTLE NOTHING
GOES A LONG WAY
© 1984 United Feature Syndicate, Inc.

WHAT WOULD YOU LIKE FOR CHRISTMAS, AUNT GUSSIE?
OH... NOTHING MUCH
JIM DAVIS
11-11

MAYBE SOMETHING FOR MY BED LIKE A LITTLE LACEY THROW PILLOW

STUFFED WITH JOHN TRAVOLTA'S CHEST HAIR

GARFIELD, YOU'RE GETTING DANGEROUSLY OVERWEIGHT
WATER
8-11
JIM DAVIS

HOW DANGEROUS CAN A LITTLE EXTRA FAT BE?
WATER

WHO, BLUB, WOULD, BLUB, HAVE, BLUB, GUESSED?
WATER

JIM DAVIS
11-5

OH NO! MY LEGS ARE TURNING TO JELLY! MY MIND IS TURNING TO MUSH! COULD IT BE A LASER?... A DEATH RAY? NO! IT'S...

MY SUNBEAM

JIM DAVIS
10-4

HERE'S ONE OF THE GREAT MYSTERIES OF THE UNIVERSE...

WHEN ODIE CLOSES HIS MOUTH, WHERE DOES HIS TONGUE GO?
© 1983 United Feature Syndicate, Inc.

I HATE IT WHEN ODIE GETS CAUGHT OUTSIDE IN THE RAIN

NOT THAT I CARE THAT MUCH FOR ODIE, MIND YOU

JIM DAVIS 10-3
© 1983 United Feature Syndicate, Inc.

I HATE MONDAY. THAT'S THE DAY PEOPLE GO BACK TO WORK, KIDS GO BACK TO SCHOOL...
JIM DAVIS

5-21

AND DIETS BEGIN
© 1984 United Feature Syndicate, Inc.

I HAVE A SLOW METABOLISM

GARFIELD, YOU'RE TOO FAT
I CAN'T HELP IT
JIM DAVIS
5-22

A REEEEEEAL SLOW METABOLISM
© 1984 United Feature Syndicate, Inc.

DO YOU KNOW WHAT I HATE ABOUT DIETS?
5-23
JIM DAVIS

EATING IS SOCIAL
ODIE

BUT WHEN YOU DIET, YOU DIET ALONE
© 1984 United Feature Syndicate, Inc.

I THINK I HAVE A WAY OUT OF THIS DIET
JIM DAVIS

I KNOW I'M TOO FAT FOR A CAT...
© 1984 United Feature Syndicate, Inc.

BUT, I'M JUST RIGHT FOR A BUMBLEBEE!
5-24

HOW GOES THE DIET, GARFIELD?
JIM DAVIS
5-26

ROAR

WHAT WAS THAT?!
THAT WAS MY STOMACH, YOU TWIT
© 1984 United Feature Syndicate,Inc.

JIM DAVIS
5-27

AYIEEEEEE!

EVERYONE'S A CRITIC
COUGH WHEEZE

HEY, GARFIELD. WE'RE GOING TO THE FARM TO VISIT DAD AND MOM THIS WEEK
3-12
JIM DAVIS

GOODO. I NEED A CHANGE OF SURROUNDINGS. I WAS GETTING BORED WITH THIS CITY LIFE

IT WILL BE NICE TO BE BORED IN THE COUNTRY FOR A CHANGE

IT'S GREAT TO BE BACK ON THE FARM, GARFIELD. NOTHING EVER CHANGES
JPM DAVPS 3-13

THE SAME OLD SURROUNDINGS, THE SAME OLD ROOM...
© 1984 United Feature Syndicate, Inc.

THE SAME OLD CHORES
THE SAME OLD MANURE

THIS PASTORAL SCENE IS NOT EXACTLY INTELLECTUALLY STIMULATING
JIM DAVIS

READ ANY GOOD BOOKS LATELY?
OINK
3-14

"OINK," HE SAYS. I REST MY CASE
"OINK" IN THE EXISTENTIAL SENSE, OF COURSE
© 1984 United Feature Syndicate, Inc.

DOC, DO YOU EVER REGRET THAT YOU STAYED ON THE FARM WHILE I WENT TO THE CITY TO LIVE IN THE LAP OF LUXURY?

NOT REALLY. DAD WILL PROBABLY WILL THE FARM TO ME, AND I'LL SELL THE ACREAGE AT A HUGE PROFIT AND RETIRE WHILE YOUNG

© 1984 United Feature Syndicate, Inc.

NEED A HIRED HAND?
GIVE ME A RESUMÉ AND THREE GOOD REFERENCES. AND MOM DOESN'T COUNT
JIM DAVIS 3-15

BEAUTIFUL SUNSET, ISN'T IT, DAD?
PURTYER THAN A LITTLE RED WAGON GOIN' UP A HILL

WHAT DOES THAT MEAN?
© 1984 United Feature Syndicate, Inc.
JIM DAVIS 3-16

OH, IT'S JUST SOMETHING YOU CITY BOYS EXPECT US FARMERS TO SAY
HOW TRUE

GARFIELD AND I MUST BE LEAVING NOW, MOM
STAY, STAY! I JUST BAKED SOME PIES
3-17
JIM DAVIS

WE GOTTA GO. COME ON, GARFIELD

SAY WHAT, STRANGER?

I'M LONELY. I THINK I'LL SEE IF I CAN FIND ARLENE
JIM DAVIS
5-14

HI THERE
YOU TWO-TIMING SWINE!

WHAT HAPPENED?

HI, ARLENE
DON'T SPEAK TO ME, YOU CAD. I SAW YOU WITH THAT OTHER WOMAN!
5-15
JIM DAVIS

OH COME ON NOW, DO I LOOK LIKE THE KIND OF GUY WHO COULD EASILY ATTRACT WOMEN?
I SUPPOSE YOU'RE RIGHT

AND JUST WHAT DO YOU MEAN BY THAT?!

JIM DAVIS
HERE IS YOUR DINNER, MY DEAR
BLAT
THIS END UP

IS THIS FOOD FRESH?
HA HA HA, WHY OF COURSE!
THIS END UP
© 1984 United Feature Syndicate, Inc.
5-16

THIS IS ONLY YESTERDAY'S NEWSPAPER
THIS END UP

AREN'T YOU GOING TO JOIN ME FOR DINNER, GARFIELD?
UH... NO THANK YOU. I'M ON A DIET
SALE
THIS END UP

A DIET?! HOW LONG HAVE YOU BEEN ON A DIET?
SALE
THIS END UP
© 1984 United Feature Syndicate, Inc.
5-17

JIM DAVIS
OH, FOR ABOUT 18 SECONDS NOW
SALE
THIS END UP

HO HUM...
5-18
JIM DAVIS

WHY DO WE SEE EACH OTHER?
IT BEATS BEING LONELY
© 1984 United Feature Syndicate, Inc.

I WAS HOPING FOR SOMETHING MORE ROMANTIC
THAT'S WAY DOWN THE LIST

5-19
JIM DAVIS

IS OUR DATE OVER?
DID IT BEGIN?
© 1984 United Feature Syndicate, Inc

SOME WOMEN DON'T APPRECIATE US STRONG, SILENT TYPES

SOME PEOPLE WONDER WHY I HATE MONDAYS
5-7

© 1984 United Feature Syndicate,Inc.
MAYBE I'M FATALISTIC
BAP
JIM DAVIS

BUT I SUSPECT I'M JUST STUPID

SCRATCH
SCRATCH
SCRATCH
5-8

© 1984 United Feature Syndicate, Inc.
WHAM!
JIM DAVIS

I'M NOT VERY FOND OF TUESDAYS, EITHER

GARFIELD! I CAN'T STRAIGHTEN UP!

ZIP
© 1984 United Feature Syndicate, Inc.
3-26

HA HA, MY TIE WAS CAUGHT IN MY ZIPPER
HELP ME
JIM DAVIS

WHIRRR
GARFIELD
JIM DAVIS
11-17

GLUP
PLOP
GARFIELD

HOW'S YOUR CAT FOOD, GARFIELD?
I COULD SAY MORE FOR THE PRESENTATION
GARFIELD

DOGS HAVE THE WORLD'S STUPIDEST TOYS. JUST LOOK AT THIS RUBBER BONE
JIM DAVIS

SIMPLE MINDS, SIMPLE PLEASURES

IT CERTAINLY DOESN'T HOLD THE SCINTILLATING INTELLECTUAL CHALLENGE OF MY FUZZY SCRATCHING POST WITH THE SPRINGY RUBBER MOUSIE
1-29
© 1983 United Feature Syndicate, Inc.

THIS IS CALLED A BIRD FEEDER, GARFIELD
JIM DAVIS
2-25

AND THIS IS CALLED PUTTING BIRDSEED INTO THE BIRD FEEDER

HE CAN CALL IT WHAT HE LIKES. I CALL IT BAITING THE TRAP
© 1983 United Feature Syndicate, Inc.

ARRRRGH!
JIM DAVIS
3-31

WHAT A HORRIBLE NIGHTMARE! I DREAMT I WAS A DOG

THANK GOODNESS IT WAS ONLY A DREAM
SCRATCH
SCRATCH
SCRATCH

GOOD MORNING, BOYS AND GIRLS
GOOD MORNING, UNCLE ROY

I LOVE YOU JUST THE WAY YOU ARE
I LOVE YOU, TOO, UNCLE ROY
© 1984 United Feature Syndicate, Inc.
JIM DAVIS 6-4

I ALSO LOVE MONDAYS
STICK IT IN YOUR EAR, UNCLE ROY

GOOD MORNING, BOYS AND GIRLS. I LOVE YOU JUST THE WAY YOU ARE
EVERYBODY LOVES UNCLE ROY

YOU ARE KIND, THOUGHTFUL, OBEDIENT AND CONSIDERATE
© 1984 United Feature Syndicate, Inc.
JIM DAVIS 6-5

NOT TO MENTION INTELLIGENT, WITTY AND CHARMING
WE ALL KNOW UNCLE ROY IS A LIAR, BUT WE DON'T CARE

HERE WE ARE IN A REAL FACTORY, BOYS AND GIRLS. LET'S SEE WHAT WE CAN LEARN...

ARRRRRGH!
WHAP! WHAP! WHAP!
© 1984 United Feature Syndicate, Inc.
JIM DAVIS 6-6

SHUT THIS ☺☆⚡✳ THING OFF
UNCLE ROY IS LEARNING NEVER TO WEAR LOOSE CLOTHING AROUND BIG MACHINERY

GOOD MORNING, BOYS AND GIRLS. YOU ARE PROBABLY WONDERING WHERE MY DOG, BOB, IS THIS MORNING

WELLLL... IT SEEMS OLD BOB BIT MR. BLUE JEANS THE MAILMAN ONCE TOO OFTEN...
© 1984 United Feature Syndicate, Inc.
JIM DAVIS 6-7

SO BOB HAS DECIDED TO MOVE TO A LOCAL RESEARCH FACILITY TO PURSUE A CAREER AS A LABORATORY ANIMAL
AND I'M FRANK SINATRA

LET'S PLAY PRETEND, BOYS AND GIRLS. LET'S PRETEND IT'S CONTRACT NEGOTIATION TIME FOR UNCLE ROY...

AND THERE ARE BIG GREEN MONSTERS WHO WANT TO TAKE UNCLE ROY OFF THE AIR...
© 1984 United Feature Syndicate, Inc.
JIM DAVIS 6-8

AND THE ONLY THING THAT CAN SAVE UNCLE ROY ARE LETTERS SAYING HOW MUCH YOU LOVE UNCLE ROY
I HATE TO SEE A GROWN MAN GROVEL

LOOK WHO'S COME TO VISIT, BOYS AND GIRLS. IT'S JERRY THE CAT. HI,JERRY
HI, UNCLE ROY

HOW ARE YOU?
I'M FINE. HOW ARE YOU?
UNCLE ROY IS GETTING PRETTY BIZARRE
JIM DAVIS 6-9
© 1984 United Feature Syndicate, Inc.

HOW'S YOUR MOTHER?
SHE'S FINE
WHO'D BE DUMB ENOUGH TO BELIEVE THERE IS A TALKING CAT?

WHY DO YOU HAVE SUCH LARGE TEETH, GARFIELD?
GARFIELD
JIM DAVIS
4-29

ALL THE BETTER TO EAT YOU WITH, MY DEAR
GARFIELD

STOP THAT!
OBVIOUSLY, SIR, YOU ARE NOT A PATRON OF THE CLASSICS
GARFIELD

I REALLY DON'T LIKE MYSELF WHEN I'M OUT OF SHAPE AND OVERWEIGHT
JIM DAVIS 9-21

WELL, THIS TIME I'M GOING TO DO SOMETHING ABOUT IT!

I'M GOING TO LOWER MY EXPECTATIONS!
© 1983 United Feature Syndicate, Inc.

HERE COMES ODIE. HIS BARK IS WORSE THAN HIS BITE
BARK! BARK!

BARK!

AND HIS BREATH IS WORSE THAN HIS BARK
JIM DAVIS 7-27

I'M TIRED OF BEING OUT OF SHAPE
GARFIELD
JIM DAVIS
9-20

I CAN'T CATCH ODIE. I CAN'T CATCH MY BREATH
GARFIELD

HECK, I CAN'T EVEN CATCH MY LUNCH
GARFIELD
© 1983 United Feature Syndicate, Inc.

GARFIELD, I KNOW YOU'RE IN MY FERN. I CAN SEE YOUR TAIL

WHAT DO YOU HAVE TO SAY FOR YOURSELF?

ARF?
JIM DAVIS
7-16

GARFIELD
JIM DAVIS
8-8

OH, NO!
GARFIELD

MY LEGS ARE SHRINKING!
GARFIELD

I'VE REALLY DONE IT THIS TIME. MY BELLY HAS OUTGROWN MY LEGS
JIM DAVIS
8-9

I GUESS THERE'S ONLY ONE THING TO DO...

GET FITTED FOR STILTS

♪ HUMMM ♫
JIM DAVIS
8-10

OH, NO!

YOU KNOW YOU'RE OVERWEIGHT WHEN YOU'RE SITTING AROUND ROCKING, AND YOU REALIZE YOU DON'T HAVE A ROCKING CHAIR
© 1983 United Feature Syndicate, Inc.

NO MORE OF THIS SNIVELING SISSY STUFF
JIM DAVIS
4-1

I'M GETTING OUT OF THIS TREE LIKE A MAN

ON THE OTHER HAND, SNIVELING DOES HAVE ITS ATTRIBUTES

I GOTTA GET OUT OF THIS TREE
JIM DAVIS
4-2

OH WELL, THEY TELL ME A CAT ALWAYS LANDS ON HIS FEET

HOWEVER, **THEY** FAILED TO MENTION THE PAIN
© 1983 United Feature Syndicate, Inc.

Dear Garfield,
What is your favorite
all-time film?
4.25
JIM DAVIS

IT'S "OLD YELLER"

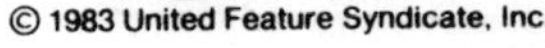

I LOVE MOVIES
WITH HAPPY
ENDINGS

LOOK AT ALL THOSE PEOPLE. ALL GOING TO WORK TO PROCESS FOOD, PRODUCE ELECTRICITY, MANUFACTURE KITTY LITTER AND SO ON

ALL JUST FOR ME

I'D THANK THEM INDIVIDUALLY, BUT THEY KNOW WHO THEY ARE
JPM DAVPS 11-14

DON'T KNOCK THOSE FLOWERS OFF THE WINDOWSILL, GARFIELD

I PUT THEM THERE TO GIVE THEM SOME SUN
JIM DAVIS
© 1982 United Feature Syndicate, Inc.

AND SOME FRESH AIR
12-6

GOOD MORNING, ODIE
JIM DAVIS
1-5-83

HEY, GET AWAY FROM JON'S STAMP COLLECTION!

TOO LATE
© 1982 United Feature Syndicate, Inc.

JIM DAVIS
4-16

I'M SORRY. DID I BRING YOU DOWN, OLD BUDDY?
LIKE A ROCK, OLD BUDDY
© 1984 United Feature Syndicate, Inc.

I'M BORED, GARFIELD
JIM DAVIS

I'M TIRED OF SEEING THE SAME OLD SCENERY. DO YOU KNOW WHAT I MEAN?
NOT REALLY...
© 1984 United Feature Syndicate, Inc.

AT LEAST YOU GET TO SEE SCENERY
4-17

THERE'S ONLY ONE PATH OUT OF THIS VALLEY OF GLOOM. THERE'S ONLY ONE SURE BET TO BEAT THE BOREDS
© 1984 United Feature Syndicate, Inc.

GARFIELD, THERE'S ONLY ONE WAY TO SHED THIS SHROUD OF GRAY WE WEAR...
JIM DAVIS 4-18

GATHER YOUR THINGS. WE'RE GOING ON VACATION!
I'M PACKED. LET'S GO!

HOW MUCH ARE THE PLANE TICKETS?... UH, DO YOU HAVE ANYTHING CHEAPER?
JIM DAVIS

THAT COULD BE FATAL!
4-19

I DON'T THINK THEY WANT OUR BUSINESS, GARFIELD
WHERE'S THE COMPETITION FOR THE LOW ROLLERS THESE DAYS?
© 1984 United Feature Syndicate, Inc.

THANK YOU VERY MUCH
JIM DAVIS

GARFIELD, I HAD TO BOOK OUR VACATION ALL THIRD-CLASS. I HOPE YOU DON'T MIND
THAT'S OKAY
4-20

IT'S STILL BETTER THAN THIS FOURTH-CLASS EXISTENCE AT HOME
© 1984 United Feature Syndicate, Inc.

LET'S BLOW THIS JOINT, GARFIELD

HANG ON!
© 1984 United Feature Syndicate, Inc.
4-21

WHERE DID YOU GO?
TO GIVE THE REFRIGERATOR A GOODBYE KISS
JIM DAVIS

I HAVEN'T SEEN A STEWARDESS IN HOURS, GARFIELD
JIM DAVIS 4-23

I'M GOING TO FIND OUT WHAT'S GOING ON AROUND HERE

© 1984 United Feature Syndicate, Inc.

EXCUSE ME, SIR. HOW'S THE SERVICE ON THIS AIRLINE?

HEY! WE'RE GETTING HUNGRY BACK HERE IN THIRD-CLASS! WHAT'S TO EAT?!
JIM DAVIS 4·24

BLAT!
BLAT!

HARDTACK AND SWILL. YUM-YUM
CONK!
CONK!

JIM DAVIS 4-25
NYAH! NYAH! NYAH! NYAH!

MIKEY, IT'S NOT NICE TO MAKE FUN OF PEOPLE, EVEN THOUGH THEY **ARE** TRAVELING IN THIRD-CLASS

NO! GARFIELD, NO!
LET ME HURT'EM JUST A LITTLE BIT!
© 1984 United Feature Syndicate, Inc.

I KNOW THIS IS JUST THE THIRD-CLASS EXIT FROM THE PLANE, GARFIELD...

BUT YOU'D THINK THEY'D GIVE US A LADDER OR SOMETHING

I WOULD LIKE YOUR CHEAPEST ROOM FOR ME AND MY CAT
YES, SIR. THAT WOULD BE THE JACK BENNY SUITE, SIR

WELL, GARFIELD, THERE'S THE BED AND THE BATHROOM'S DOWN THE HALL. ANY QUESTIONS?
YES...

JIM DAVIS 4-27
WHERE ARE **YOU** GOING TO SLEEP?

ALL I HAVE TO DO IS UNPACK, GARFIELD, AND WE'LL BE READY FOR SOME REST AND RELAXATION
CLICK

ARRRRGH! NOT ANOTHER PET TO TAKE CARE OF!
JIM DAVIS 4-28
© 1984 United Feature Syndicate, Inc.

I DON'T THINK I CAN TAKE ANY MORE SURPRISES
THEN DON'T LOOK AT WHAT ODIE DID TO YOUR SPORT JACKET

HEY, GARFIELD! ARE YOU READY TO GO PLAY GOLF?

© 1984 United Feature Syndicate, Inc.
JIM DAVIS

AREN'T YOU COMING?
ON SECOND THOUGHT, I THINK I'D RATHER STAY IN THE ROOM AND WATCH THE SINK BACK-UP
4-30

ODIE! GET AWAY FROM THAT TREE! GARFIELD! GET OUT OF THAT SAND TRAP!

WOULD YOU MIND OBSERVING PROPER GOLF ETIQUETTE THERE, MISTER?
JIM DAVIS 5-1
© 1984 United Feature Syndicate, Inc.

I'M SORRY, BUT MY PETS ARE DRIVING ME NUTS
IT'S THE OUTFIT I'M TALKING ABOUT

JIM DAVIS
CRACK!
5-2

OH, NO! I HIT AN OLD LADY IN THE HEAD AND KNOCKED HER OUT COLD!

WHAT SHOULD I DO, GARFIELD?!
I'D STRAIGHTEN THAT LEFT ARM A BIT AND TURN THAT RIGHT HAND OVER MORE

JIM DAVIS

ROWR!
© 1984 United Feature Syndicate, Inc.
5-3

GARFIELD! WHAT ARE YOU DOING IN THAT SAND TRAP?
SQUATTING ON A SANDBUR, THANK YOU

WELL, BOYS, IT'S BEEN A NICE VACATION, BUT IT'S TIME TO HEAD HOME

GOOD HEAVENS! WHAT HAPPENED TO YOU GUYS?!

JIM DAVIS 5-4
ODIE DISCOVERED HOW TO DIAL ROOM SERVICE
BURP

HERE WE ARE! HOME SWEET HOME!

ARRRGH!
© 1984 United Feature Syndicate, Inc.

OKAY, WHO LEFT THE FAUCET RUNNING?!
I DIDN'T WANT MY SPONGE COLLECTION TO DRY OUT
JIM DAVIS 5-5

JIM DAVIS

1-4-84

OH,NO! IT'S THE OLD "DISGUISE THE TONGUE AS A LOAF OF FRENCH BREAD" TRICK!
© 1983 United Feature Syndicate, Inc.

WATER
JIM DAVIS
7-14

SLUP
SLUP
SLUP
WATER

DROOL
FUEL
WATER

RATS! IT'S THE DOG NEXT DOOR!
JIM DAVIS
8-13

EVER HAD A NIGHTMARE COME TRUE?

IT'S HARD TO BELIEVE I'M GOING TO BE FIVE YEARS OLD THIS SUNDAY
JIM DAVIS
6-14

SHUCKS, GOLLY, GEE-WHIZ, RATSO

I'M GOING TO HAVE TO START WATCHING MY LANGUAGE
© 1983 United Feature Syndicate, Inc.

GARFIELD, I HOPE THE SUN SHINES ON YOUR BIRTHDAY

WHAT A NICE THING TO SAY

JIM DAVIS
6-15
I'M GOING CAMPING
I DIDN'T NEED THAT

JIM DAVIS
6-16

MOTHER NATURE HAS CERTAINLY BEEN KIND TO YOU, GARFIELD

I WISH I COULD SAY THE SAME FOR FATHER TIME
© 1983 United Feature Syndicate, Inc.

IT'S NEARLY MIDNIGHT ON A MONDAY
JPM DAVPS 4-9

I CAN'T BELIEVE IT! NOTHING BAD HAS HAPPENED TO ME ALL DAY

COO-COO!

WATCH THIS. IT'S THE OLD RUBBER BONE GAG

SHOOP!

PRACTICAL JOKES ARE WASTED ON THE STUPID
4-10
JIM DAVIS

JIM DAVIS 4-11
SQUIT

BLAT

UNNNNGH! HELP! HELP! THE ALIEN IS SUCKING MY BRAIN DRY!
GARFIELD HAS RAISED PLAYING WITH FOOD TO AN ART FORM

RISE AND SHINE, GARFIELD!
3-28
JIM DAVIS

GARFIELD?

TIME TO WASH MY BLANKEY. WHAT SAY?
CLUNK CLUNK
© 1984 United Feature Syndicate, Inc.

BE A GOOD BOY AND FETCH THE MORNING PAPER, GARFIELD
3-29
JIM DAVIS

YES, MASTER. I AM AT YOUR BECK AND CALL, MASTER

WHY CAN'T I HAVE A NORMAL HOUSE CAT LIKE EVERYONE ELSE?
© 1984 United Feature Syndicate, Inc.

I NEED A BRAIN FOR MY MASTER
JIM DAVIS
3-30

A BRAIN, I NEED A BRAIN FOR MY MASTER
© 1984 United Feature Syndicate, Inc.

AH, COFFEE
JIM DAVIS
3-31

BEING A HUNCHBACK IS GOING TO TAKE SOME GETTING USED TO

OH, NO! DON'T MAKE ME DO IT! ANYTHING BUT THAT!
JIM DAVIS

TURN BACK! TURN BACK!
© 1983 United Feature Syndicate, Inc.
12-12

SOMETIMES, A CAT'S FEET JUST GOTTA CLIMB

HERE I AM, STUCK UP A TREE. THINGS COULDN'T BE WORSE
JIM DAVIS
12-13

OKAY, OKAY, **NOW** THINGS COULDN'T BE WORSE
© 1983 United Feature Syndicate, Inc.

BOOM

I MAY BE STRANDED UP A TREE...
JIM DAVIS

BUT AT LEAST I'M ON A STURDY LIMB
12-14

THE STORY OF MY LIFE

HEY, FATSO. WHAT DOES A BIRD LIKE YOU EAT?
JIM DAVIS
12-15

CATS

CHIRP CHIRP

THIS ISN'T SAFE
JIM DAVIS
12-16

SHOO! SHOO! SOMEBODY MIGHT GET HURT!

TOING!

A WAY DOWN! ALL I HAVE TO DO IS DIVE INTO THAT BIRDBATH
12-17

7.0
6.5
JIM DAVIS

BARK!
BARK!
BARK!

ODIE ISN'T REALLY STUPID
BONK

HE'S JUST CHASED ONE TOO MANY PARKED CARS
7-18
JIM DAVIS

ARE YOU GOING TO SLEEP ALL DAY, GARFIELD?
LET ME CHECK MY SOCIAL CALENDAR
7-27
JIM DAVIS

LET'S SEE...THERE'S HIGH TEA WITH THE QUEEN OF ENGLAND TOMORROW, BUT NOTHING TODAY

ASK A STUPID QUESTION...
Z
© 1984 United Feature Syndicate,Inc.

YAWN
WHAT A GREAT NIGHT'S SLEEP!
JIM DAVIS
7-28

I'M READY TO ATTACK A FRESH NEW DAY

GOOD EVENING, GARFIELD
WHAT'S ON THE LATE MOVIE?

IT'S MONDAY OUT THERE. I FEEL IT IN THE AIR. I HATE MONDAYS
JIM DAVIS
4-2

I'M SURE THE WORLD WILL END ON A MONDAY... AT LEAST I HOPE IT DOES

IT WOULD BE A SHAME TO END THE WORLD RIGHT BEFORE A WEEKEND

POOKY, WHERE ARE YOU? OH, NO! MY TEDDY BEAR IS MISSING
JIM DAVIS
4-3

THIS HAS THE MAKINGS OF A CLASSIC MYSTERY. I ALREADY HAVE SOME PRIME SUSPECTS

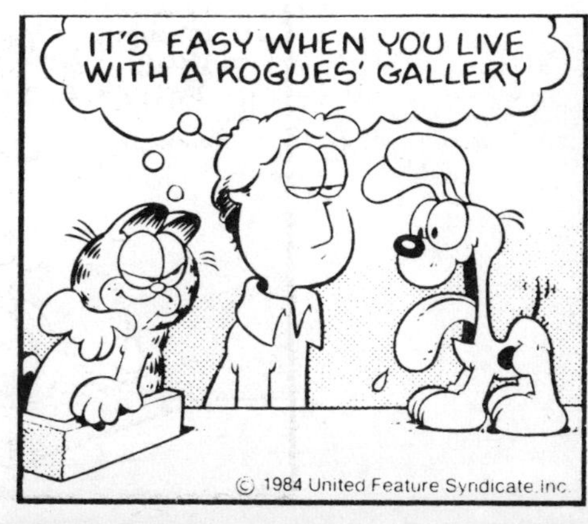
IT'S EASY WHEN YOU LIVE WITH A ROGUES' GALLERY
© 1984 United Feature Syndicate, inc.

THERE MUST BE A CLUE TO POOKY'S DISAPPEARANCE HERE SOMEWHERE...
4-5

AHA! COULD THIS BE A TELLTALE TRAIL OF TEDDY BEAR HAIR?
© 1984 United Feature Syndicate, Inc.
© JIM DAVIS

EVEN IF IT ISN'T, THAT WAS A PRETTY NIFTY BIT OF ALLITERATION

HELLO, WHAT'S THIS? JUST AS MY TEDDY BEAR DISAPPEARS, THIS SACK MYSTERIOUSLY APPEARS...
JIM DAVIS

SOMETHING SMELLS FISHY HERE

4-6

I SUSPECT ODIE OF KIDNAPPING POOKY. WATCH HIM CRUMBLE UNDER MY KEEN QUESTIONING
JIM DAVIS
4-4

WHERE WERE YOU ON THE EVENING OF APRIL 1 ?!

WHAT AM I DOING? ODIE DOESN'T EVEN KNOW WHERE HE IS NOW

AHA! JON! IT WAS YOU WHO KIDNAPPED POOKY!
JIM DAVIS

OBVIOUSLY, SENSING I WAS HOT ON HIS TRAIL AND FEARING MY WRATH, HE'S DECIDED TO RETURN POOKY AND THROW HIMSELF ON THE MERCY OF THE COURT

4-7

I HAD YOUR TEDDY BEAR CLEANED, GARFIELD
SIGH... THANK YOU
© 1984 United Feature Syndicate, Inc.

GARFIELD, SOMETIMES I THINK YOU DON'T LIKE IT WHEN I HAVE DATES
ABSOLUTELY
JIM DAVIS
1-21

DATING LEADS TO MARRIAGE. MARRIAGE LEADS TO CHILDREN

AND DO YOU KNOW WHAT CHILDREN DO TO CATS?
© 1983 United Feature Syndicate, Inc.

JON BOY! MOM BOY! DOC BOY! HOW ARE YOU?
OH BOY

DOC BOY!
DON'T CALL ME "DOC BOY"

YOUR BROTHER, DOC, HAS COME BACK TO WORK ON THE FARM. HE'S HERE NOW
JIM DAVIS
5-17

WHAT BRINGS YOU TO THE FARM, JON?
I PROMISED GARFIELD SOME GOOD HOME COOKING
JIM DAVIS
5-18

WHAT WOULD YOU BOYS LIKE FOR BREAKFAST?

MY GUESS IS GARFIELD WOULD LIKE SOME HAM AND EGGS
© 1983 United Feature Syndicate, Inc.

JIM DAVIS
DOC, YOU'RE LOOKING MORE LIKE DAD ALL THE TIME

YOU TAKE THAT BACK!

© 1983 United Feature Syndicate, Inc.
5-19
SMACK!
HUSH UP, BOY
THE THREE STOOGES LIVE

YOU KNOW, DOC, FOR BROTHERS, WE DON'T LOOK MUCH ALIKE
JIM DAVIS 5-20

IT'S HARD TO BELIEVE WE CAME FROM THE SAME PLACE

YOU MEAN, THE FARM?
THE FUNNY FARM MAYBE

TAKE CARE NOW
SEE YOU SOON
DON'T BE A STRANGER
JIM DAVIS

SO LONG!
BYE BYE!
BYE NOW
SEE YUH

I CAN'T BELIEVE THE FUSS THEY MAKE OVER GOING TO BED
YOU HAVE A VERY CLOSE FAMILY
5-21

JIM DAVIS

YOU KNOW IT'S MONDAY WHEN YOU FIND SHARKS CIRCLING IN YOUR WATER BOWL
GARFIELD
© 1981 United Feature Syndicate, Inc
8-3

JIM DAVIS
5-18

CHUG!

YOU'RE A REAL BEAR UNTIL YOU'VE HAD YOUR FIRST CUP OF COFFEE, AREN'T YOU?
AND THEN I'M THE SWEETEST SO-AND-SO AROUND
© 1982 United Feature Syndicate, Inc.

YOU SLEEP TOO MUCH, GARFIELD
7-23
JIM DAVIS

© 1984 United Feature Syndicate, Inc.
SOMETIMES I DO FEEL BAD ABOUT SLEEPING SO MUCH

WHAT WITH ALL THE INSOMNIACS IN CHINA

AND NOW, A WORD FROM OUR SPONSOR
7-16
JIM DAVIS

HEY, AMERICA, HERE'S A CAT FOOD WE BET YOUR CAT WILL LOVE
© 1984 United Feature Syndicate, Inc.

YOU'RE ON

GOOD MORNING, OLD BUDDY
7-17
JIM DAVIS

ARRRGH!
THAT'S ONLY A PIECE OF LINT, GARFIELD

IT SURE DOES A GREAT SPIDER IMPRESSION

Garfield
Strikes Again

JIM DAVIS

RR

OKAY, WHO LOOSENED THE TOP ON MY SALTSHAKER?!
JIM DAVIS

GARFIELD, THAT WASN'T VERY NICE
YOU'RE RIGHT. THAT WASN'T VERY NICE

BUT IT WAS EXTREMELY FUNNY
1-5-84

WHO'S THAT PANTING AT MY DOOR?
JIM DAVIS 3-5

HONK
HONK

OH, GOOD MORNING, ODIE
HONK

YAWN
3-6
JIM DAVIS

GASP!

WAKING UP TO MY OWN BAD BREATH IS BAD ENOUGH, BUT SOMEONE ELSE'S IS UNBEARABLE

I AM PROUD TO BE A PET. PETS LEND A TOUCH OF ELEGANCE TO A HOME
SLUP SLUP
JIM DAVIS
© 1984 United Feature Syndicate, Inc.

I AM PROUD TO BE A CAT
SLUP SLUP
3-7

OKAY, GET REVVED UP THERE, ODIE
3-8
JIM DAVIS

GO!

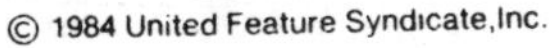

I LOVE TOYS THAT DON'T NEED BATTERIES

JIM DAVIS
3-9

CRINKLE

MAY I HAVE SOME OF THAT CANDY BAR?
HERE, TAKE IT
ICH

3-10

I DECLARE THIS STEAK THE SOVEREIGN PROPERTY OF GARFIELD, THE CAT!
JIM DAVIS

I'VE NEVER HAD MY DINNER ANNEXED BEFORE
AND YOU MAY NEVER SEE IT ALIVE AGAIN
© 1984 United Feature Syndicate, Inc.

GIMME THOSE COOKIES
3-27
JIM DAVIS

HIYA! HUT!
KONK!
PUNT!
© 1984 United Feature Syndicate,Inc.

I'D TURN HER IN, BUT WHO'D ADMIT TO BEING MANGLED BY A GIRL SCOUT?

I WONDER HOW FAST I CAN RUN
JIM DAVIS
1-30

I WONDER WHAT WOULD HAPPEN IF I HIT THIS KITTY DOOR AT MACH 2

I WONDER IF KILLING A MAILMAN IS A FEDERAL OFFENSE

I LOVE ATTACKING THE MAILMAN. SOME DAYS I SCRATCH HIM. SOME DAYS I BITE HIM. SOME DAYS I TRIP HIM

TODAY I'M TRYING SOMETHING NEW
♪

I'M HUMILIATING HIM
JIM DAVIS
1-31

♪
JIM DAVIS 2-1

ARRRGH!
B-B-B-B

WHEN HE COMES AROUND, HE'LL THANK ME FOR BREAKING UP THE MONOTONY OF HIS DREARY JOB
© 1984 United Feature Syndicate, Inc.

COME ON, MAILMAN, DELIVER THAT MAIL
JIM DAVIS
2-2

AND WHEN YOU DO, I'M GOING TO LEAP ON YOU AND ALL THAT WILL BE LEFT WILL BE YOUR MAILBAG AND THAT SILLY-LOOKING HAT OF YOURS

HAS THE MAILMAN COME YET, GARFIELD?
NO, HE'S STILL STANDING AT THE END OF THE SIDEWALK SOBBING
© 1984 United Feature Syndicate, Inc.

SLAM!
JIM DAVIS
2-3

RATS! I MISSED HIM

APPARENTLY, NO ONE EVER TOLD HIM TO LOOK BOTH WAYS BEFORE CROSSING THE STREET
SCREECH
© 1984 United Feature Syndicate,Inc.

I'LL CUT THE LASAGNA IN TWO PIECES, AND YOU TAKE FIRST PICK
JIM DAVIS
5-21

IT'S GETTING COLD, GARFIELD
© 1982 United Feature Syndicate, Inc.

YOU REALLY SHOULD THINK ABOUT JOGGING, GARFIELD. IT'S 50% MENTAL, YOU KNOW
IT IS?
JIM DAVIS
5-20

GREAT!

JOG, JOG, JOG. JOG, JOG, JOG. PANT, PANT. SWEAT
I'LL WORK ON THE OTHER 50% SOME OTHER TIME
© 1982 United Feature Syndicate, Inc.

BE A GOOD BOY AND FETCH THE MAIL, GARFIELD
OUI, MON CAPITAINE
2-4
JIM DAVIS

RIP
ROWR
CLOBBER
BLAP

DID YOU HURT HIM BAD?
OH, JUST A FEW LACERATIONS, ABRASIONS AND INTERNAL INJURIES. I WAS IN A GOOD MOOD

BRINNNG!
JIM DAVIS
1-3-83

WHAM!

BRINNNG!

GARFIELD, WHY IS IT CATS LIKE TO GET OUT AT NIGHT?
4-27
JIM DAVIS

THAT'S WHEN WE LIKE TO SING ON FENCES

IN THE DAYLIGHT, WE'D BE EASY TARGETS
© 1983 United Feature Syndicate, Inc.

LET US EXAMINE A PET PHENOMENON CALLED THE "RIPS"
JIM DAVIS
1-19

THAT'S WHEN YOUR PETS RACE AROUND THE HOUSE FOR NO APPARENT REASON

OTHER THAN TO MANGLE THE FAMILY CAT
© 1984 United Feature Syndicate, Inc.

YOU BOYS STOP RACING AROUND
JIM DAVIS
1·20

GARFIELD, SLOW DOWN!

OKAY

WOULD YOU LIKE TO GO FOR A WALK, ODIE ?
JIM DAVIS
1-21

LET'S SEE... I NEED A LEASH

YOU STAY OUT OF THIS
© 1984 United Feature Syndicate,Inc.

JIM DAVIS
12-9

MY NEWSPAPER! YOU CHEWED UP MY NEWSPAPER!

IT'S THINGS LIKE THIS THAT MAKE ME WONDER IF YOU SHOULD BRING IN THE PAPER AT ALL
PRECISELY
POO
© 1982 United Feature Syndicate, Inc.

I GOTTA BEAT THAT FLY TO MY FOOD!
JIM DAVIS
3-22

I WIN!

YOU LOSE, FELLA
POO
GARFIELD
© 1984 United Feature Syndicate, Inc.

JIM DAVIS

WHEW
3-23
© 1984 United Feature Syndicate, Inc.

BOO!

♪
JIM DAVIS

REARRR!
© 1984 United Feature Syndicate,Inc.
3-24

IT'S THE OLD "BRING IN THE REINFORCEMENTS" TRICK

HERE YOU GO, GARFIELD. TAKE A BIG BITE
JIM DAVIS
11-21

OH NO!

JUST KIDDING
© 1983 United Feature Syndicate, Inc.

GARFIELD, I THINK YOU'RE TOO MEAN TO ODIE
JIM DAVIS 6-25

I NEVER WANT TO SEE YOU HIT HIM AGAIN
OH, VERY WELL

KONK!

I'M GOING TO THE STORE, GARFIELD. IF YOU LAY A PAW ON ODIE, I'LL SPANK YOU

BOING
JIM DAVIS
6-26

GARFIELD, I SWEAR YOU'VE DONE EVERYTHING TO ODIE A CAT COULD DO TO A DOG
AU CONTRAIRE
JIM DAVIS

PLINK
© 1984 United Feature Syndicate, Inc.
6-27

NEVER UNDERESTIMATE ME

HEY, ODIE!
I FOUND
YOUR NOSE!

LET ME PUT
IT ON FOR
YOU, PAL
SQUIK
SQUIK

VERY NICE. I LIKE YOU
AS A RAT TERRIER
SNIFF
JIM DAVIS
6-28

WELL, WELL, WELL. I SEE YOU'RE EATING MY FOOD, ODIE. NOW WHAT ARE WE GOING TO DO WITH YOU?
GARFIELD
JIM DAVIS
6-29

WE ARE GOING TO KICK YOU INTO NEXT WEEK! THAT'S WHAT WE'RE GOING TO DO!
PUNT
GARFIELD

WHERE'S ODIE?
SOMEWHERE OVER SATURDAY
© 1984 United Feature Syndicate, Inc.

LUNCH ISN'T THE SAME WITHOUT ODIE. HE ALWAYS SLIPS UP BEHIND ME, BARKS LOUDLY AND MAKES ME FALL INTO MY FOOD
GARFIELD
JIM DAVIS 6-30

I GUESS I'LL JUST HAVE TO MAKE DO
GARFIELD

BLUT
GARFIELD

I'M WORKING UP A ROUTINE FOR THE FENCE TONIGHT, POOKY. TELL ME WHAT YOU THINK OF IT
JIM DAVIS
7-4

I KNEW A TEDDY BEAR WHO WAS SO UGLY, EVEN THE TIDE WOULDN'T TAKE IT OUT

BLAT!

GOOD EVENING, LADIES AND GERMS. I'D LIKE YOU TO MEET POOKY, MY GAG WRITER
JIM DAVIS
7-5

SPLAT

WELCOME TO SHOW BIZ, KID

JUMP THROUGH THE HOOP, POOKY
JIM DAVIS

HEY, GARFIELD. WHAT'S HAPPENING?
I'M PRETENDING TO TEACH POOKY TRICKS

7-6
© 1984 United Feature Syndicate,Inc.

BUTTERFLIES ARE VERSATILE. THEY CAN CARESS THE AIR
JIM DAVIS 7-7

THEY CAN KISS THE DEW FROM THE FLOWERS

AND THEY CAN EMBED THEMSELVES IN RADIATORS
FWAP!

I HAVE THIS NAGGING FEELING I'M FORGETTING SOMETHING
JIM DAVIS
7-2

WHUMP!

OH YES, I FORGOT I KICKED ODIE INTO NEXT WEEK, LAST WEEK

Z
JIM DAVIS
2-21

BARK!

© 1983 United Feature Syndicate, Inc.

I SEE YOU'RE BRINGING THE MAIL IN WITH YOUR USUAL CARE
JIM DAVIS
12-8

THIS LETTER SAYS, "DO NOT FOLD, SPINDLE OR MUTILATE"

IT DIDN'T SAY ANYTHING ABOUT "MAUL"

AWK!
JIM DAVIS
3-19

I LOVE CHASING BIRDS

EXCEPT WHEN THEY DO THAT

BONK!
RATS!
3-20
JIM DAVIS

DOUBLE RATS!

AND, OF COURSE, TRIPLE RATS

HEH HEH
RATTLE RATTLE
JIM DAVIS
12-26

CATS HAVE SUCH ACTIVE IMAGINATIONS. I WONDER WHAT'S GOING ON IN GARFIELD'S MIND RIGHT NOW

WELL... HERE I AM, IN A BROWN PAPER BAG
© 1983 United Feature Syndicate, Inc.

INTERESTING
12-27
JIM DAVIS

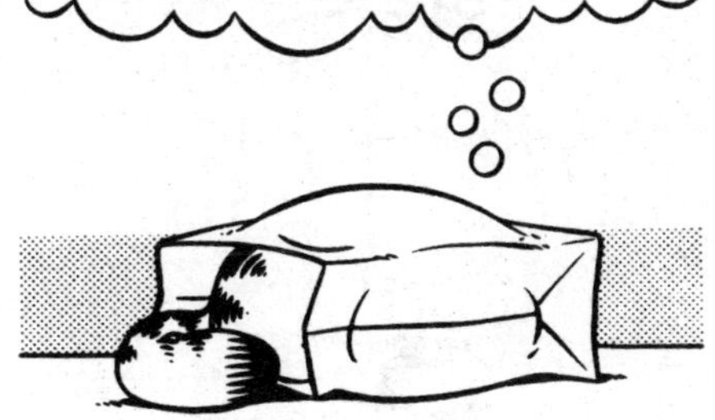
RESIDING IN A BROWN PAPER BAG GIVES ONE AN ALL-NEW PERSPECTIVE ON ONE'S SELF

I FEEL LIKE A DIRTY MAGAZINE
© 1983 United Feature Syndicate, Inc.

THIS BAG NEEDS EYEHOLES
12-28
JIM DAVIS

RIP
RUSTLE
RUSTLE

SOMETHING'S NOT RIGHT HERE

GOT MY SACK, GOT MY EYEHOLES, WHAT MORE COULD A CAT NEED?
JIM DAVIS
12-29

ARRRRGH!

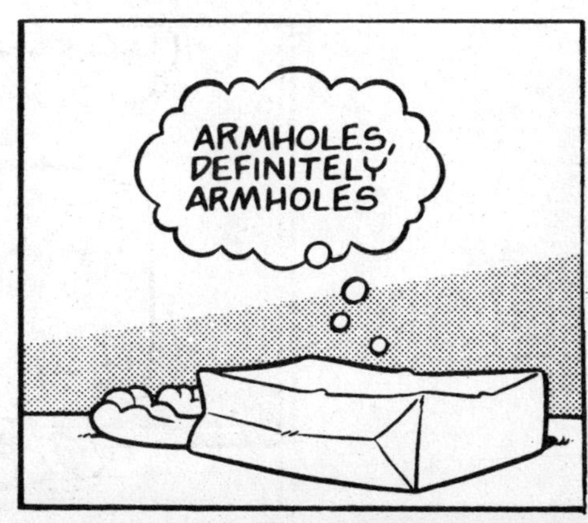
ARMHOLES, DEFINITELY ARMHOLES

AWK! THERE'S SOMEONE IN THIS BAG WITH ME
JIM DAVIS
12-30

OH, IT'S YOU

HELLO, BELLYBUTTON

FFFFF
JIM DAVIS
12-31

POW!

I DIDN'T KNOW YOU WERE IN THE BAG, GARFIELD. I WAS PLAYING A TRICK ON ODIE
AT LEAST I DIED FOR A GOOD CAUSE

I AM ABSOLUTELY NOT GETTING OUT OF BED TODAY
JIM DAVIS
5-9

HEY, GARFIELD, THERE'S A SPIDER ON YOUR BLANKET

I KEEP FORGETTING WE LIVE IN A GENERATION WITHOUT ABSOLUTES

I'LL TEACH HIM TO BE A SPIDER!
STOMP STOMP STOMP
STOMP STOMP
5-10

HE WON'T HAVE THE GUTS TO DO THAT AGAIN
© 1984 United Feature Syndicate, Inc.
JIM DAVIS

BETTER SAFE THAN SORRY
STOMP STOMP
STOMP STOMP STOMP

LOOK AT THIS
JIM DAVIS
5-11

A CAT STROKING HIS OWNER!

WHY SO AFFECTIONATE, GARFIELD?
I JUST SQUASHED A SPIDER
© 1984 United Feature Syndicate, Inc.

GARFIELD
5-12
JIM DAVIS

SLUG

BIG DAY
GARFIELD

I HATE MONDAYS
GARFIELD, I DON'T KNOW WHY YOU HATE MONDAYS SO MUCH
5-28
JIM DAVIS

BLAT!

SEE?!!!
© 1984 United Feature Syndicate, Inc.

GOOD MORNING, GARFIELD
5-29
JIM DAVIS

I MADE YOUR COFFEE JUST LIKE YOU LIKE IT

STRONG
© 1984 United Feature Syndicate, Inc.

OH SHUCKS, I JUST SPILLED THE ONLY CUP OF COFFEE WE HAVE IN THE HOUSE
JIM DAVIS
5-30

1-23
JIM DAVIS

GOOD MORNING, GARFIELD. IT'S ME, NERMAL. I'M YOUNG AND GOOD-LOOKING AND YOU'RE NOT

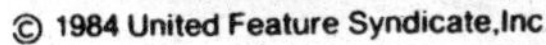

I DIDN'T NEED THAT

CAN I GET YOU ANYTHING FOR BREAKFAST, GARFIELD?
1-24
JIM DAVIS

YEAH, HOW ABOUT A BIG GLASS OF FRESHLY-SQUEEZED KITTEN JUICE?

YOU DON'T LIKE ME, DO YOU?
© 1984 United Feature Syndicate, Inc.

HOW CUTE! NERMAL BROUGHT ME MY NEWSPAPER
JIM DAVIS
1-25

AND MY SLIPPERS AND MY PIPE! WHAT MORE COULD A MAN WANT?

HOW ABOUT A WOMAN?
© 1984 United Feature Syndicate, Inc.

LET'S GET YOU INTO TROUBLE, NERMAL
COOKIES
1-26
JIM DAVIS

LOOK IN THE COOKIE JAR! LOOK IN THE COOKIE JAR!
NO, YOU CAN'T HAVE A COOKIE, GARFIELD. YOU'LL SPOIL DINNER
COOKIES

THANKS FOR THE COOKIES
JEFF WOULD HAVE KNOWN WHAT LASSIE WAS TALKING ABOUT
COOKIES

ODIE
JIM DAVIS
1-27

BLUT, BLUT!
ODIE

CALL IT CRUEL. CALL IT JUVENILE. I CALL IT ASSERTING MYSELF
ODIE

I HATE TO BOTHER YOU, SIR, BUT YOU PUT INSUFFICIENT POSTAGE ON YOUR PACKAGE

WHAT PACKAGE?

THIS KITTEN YOU'RE SENDING TO ABU DHABI
GARFIELD
JIM DAVIS 1-28

HEY, GARFIELD, IT SAYS HERE PEOPLE CAN PERFORM SUPER-HUMAN FEATS OF STRENGTH DURING PERIODS OF GREAT STRESS
2-6

WHAT BALONEY!

BY THE WAY, I'M TAKING YOU TO THE VET TODAY
JIM DAVIS

YOU CAN'T HIDE FROM ME FOREVER, GARFIELD. I'M GOING TO FIND YOU AND TAKE YOU TO THE VET
JIM DAVIS

YOU MAY BE SNEAKY, BUT I'M SNEAKIER

"SNEAKY" IS MY MIDDLE NAME
2-7
© 1984 United Feature Syndicate, Inc.

GARFIELD CAN'T RESIST LASAGNA, AND WHEN HE COMES TO EAT IT, I'M GOING TO CATCH HIM AND TAKE HIM TO THE VET
JIM DAVIS
2-8

SMACK
GULP
SLURP

THAT CAT HAS THE LONGEST LIPS I'VE EVER SEEN

NOW WHERE COULD GARFIELD BE?
Biscuits
COOKIES
2-9
JIM DAVIS

HE'S NOT IN THE COOKIES, AND HE CERTAINLY WOULDN'T BE IN THE DOGGIE BISCUITS
Biscuits
COOKIES

IT'S A GOOD THING I CAN'T READ
POO!
Biscuits
COOKIES
© 1984 United Feature Syndicate,Inc.

AHA! THERE YOU ARE, GARFIELD! YOU'RE GOING TO THE VET NOW
JIM DAVIS

© 1984 United Feature Syndicate,Inc.

SORRY, ODIE
SMACK
2-10

I WISH I COULD FIND GARFIELD'S HIDING PLACE SO I COULD TAKE HIM TO THE VET
JIM DAVIS
2-11

HE'S SURE HIDING IN A GOOD PLACE

A GOOD PLACE--
NOT A SMART PLACE--
BUT A GOOD PLACE

IF PEOPLE HAD HAIR ALL OVER THEIR BODIES, WOULD THEY WEAR CLOTHING ?
JIM DAVIS

2-14

PROBABLY NOT

WHAT WOULD HAPPEN IF PEOPLE WERE CATS AND CATS WERE PEOPLE?

THAT'S AN EASY ONE

DOGS WOULD SOON BECOME EXTINCT

I WAS WONDERING, GARFIELD...
© 1984 United Feature Syndicate, Inc.

WHAT IF BEING FAT WERE CONSIDERED ATTRACTIVE?

JIM DAVIS 2·16
WHAT DO YOU MEAN, "WHAT IF," BOZO?

THIS IS YOUR CONSCIENCE SPEAKING. DON'T YOU DARE PUSH ODIE OFF THE TABLE! THAT WOULD BE INHUMANE AND CRUEL
GARFIELD

THEN YOU PUSH HIM OFF
POKE!
GARFIELD
2-21

© 1984 United Feature Syndicate, Inc.
THAT WAS KIND OF FUN
RFIELD
JIM DAVIS

I WONDER WHAT LIFE WOULD BE LIKE IF WE NEVER HAD TO EAT

IT WOULD TAKE SOME GETTING USED TO

FOR A TIME, MOTHERS WOULD FIX THEIR FAMILIES THREE SQUARE NOTHINGS A DAY
JIM DAVIS 2·17

WHAT IF THERE WERE NEVER A LEONARDO DA VINCI?

THAT WOULD BE AWFUL!

JIM DAVIS 2·18
THE DA VINCI KIDS WOULD HAVE BEEN ORPHANS

I HATE MONDAYS
JIM DAVIS
2-20

THIS IS YOUR CONSCIENCE SPEAKING. IT'S NOT NICE TO HATE MONDAYS. LOOK AT IT AS STARTING A FRESH WEEK WITH A CLEAN SLATE

I HATE MONDAYS

WHAT ODIE NEEDS IS A GOOD KICK

UH-OH! NAP ATTACK!
© 1984 United Feature Syndicate, Inc.

I DON'T EVEN WANT TO KNOW
Z
7-24
JIM DAVIS

WHY DO YOU FOLLOW ME AROUND, CONSCIENCE?
IF I DON'T, YOU WON'T BE VERY NICE

IF I PUT THIS CORK IN YOUR BOTTLE WOULD YOU BE TRAPPED?
YES, BUT THAT WOULDN'T BE VERY NICE

THAT WASN'T VERY NICE
© 1984 United Feature Syndicate, Inc.
JIM DAVIS
2-22

NOW THAT MY CONSCIENCE IS TRAPPED IN THIS BOTTLE, I CAN WALK AWAY AND ENJOY MYSELF
2·23

THAT'S OKAY, GO AHEAD, HAVE FUN, DON'T WORRY ABOUT ME. I'LL JUST SIT HERE IN THE DARK... ALL ALONE
© 1984 United Feature Syndicate, Inc.
JIM DAVIS

YOU'RE VERY GOOD
ONE OF THE BEST

LET'S HAVE SOME FUN, GARFIELD. TAKE ONE STEP BACK
OKAY
JIM DAVIS
2-24

I THOUGHT CONSCIENCES WERE SUPPOSED TO BE NICE!
I'M ON BREAK

I HAVE MY CONSCIENCE TRAPPED IN THIS BOTTLE. I'LL JUST SET IT BY JON
JIM DAVIS
2-25

GET A HAIRCUT

EVERY MORNING FOR NEARLY SIX YEARS NOW, I FIX RAISIN TOAST FOR GARFIELD

JIM DAVIS 6-12
HE LOVES HIS RAISIN TOAST

WHAT'S IN THE DRAWER?
A SIX-YEAR SUPPLY OF RAISINS

ROWR
5-31

WHOCK!

GARFIELD, WHERE DID THE FLOWERS COME FROM?!
WELL, WHY DON'T WE JUST READ THE NOTE?
JIM DAVIS

YOU LIKE TO SCRATCH THINGS, DON'T YOU, GARFIELD?
DOES A CHICKEN LIKE TO PECK? SURE I DO!
JIM DAVIS
6-1

GOOD! SCRATCH MY BACK

NO CLAWS! NO CLAWS!
IF I DIDN'T USE CLAWS, I WOULDN'T BE SCRATCHING, NOW WOULD I?
© 1984 United Feature Syndicate, Inc.

SCRATCH HIGHER, GARFIELD
JIM DAVIS

HIGHER!

6-2

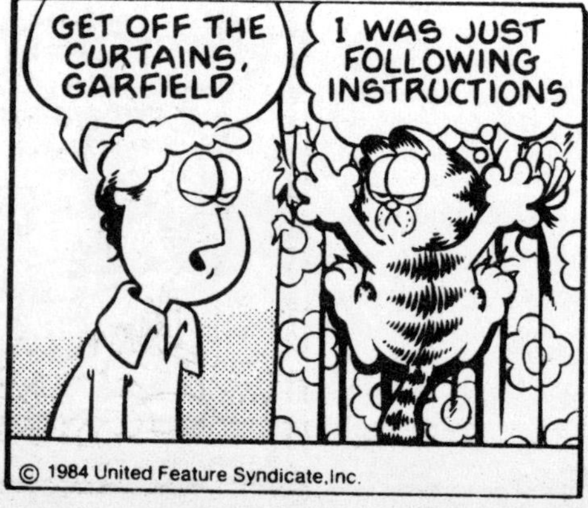
GET OFF THE CURTAINS, GARFIELD
I WAS JUST FOLLOWING INSTRUCTIONS
© 1984 United Feature Syndicate, Inc.

JIM DAVIS 8-15

RIIIP!

CRUELTY IS SECOND NATURE TO THAT CAT
© 1983 United Feature Syndicate, Inc.

BONK!
BONK!
JIM DAVIS

BONK!
BONK!
11-2

ODIE'S GOING TO HAVE TO LEARN TO WALK ONE OF THESE DAYS
© 1983 United Feature Syndicate, Inc.

I WANTED TO BUY YOU ANOTHER BED, GARFIELD. BUT THE ONLY SIZES THEY CAME IN WERE SMALL, MEDIUM AND LARGE
GARFIELD
10-5
JIM DAVIS

THEY DIDN'T HAVE SHOWBOAT!
GARFIELD

A QUICK WIT IS BEST ACCOMPANIED BY QUICK REFLEXES
© 1983 United Feature Syndicate, Inc.

JIM DAVIS 6-11

DON'T YOU DARE
I DON'T KNOW WHAT YOU'RE TALKING ABOUT

STOP BEGGING, GARFIELD. YOU MAY HAVE ANY FOOD THAT FALLS ON THE FLOOR

I HATE YOU
I CAN LIVE WITH THAT
JIM DAVIS 4-13

COOKIES
JIM DAVIS
6-30

COOKIES

COOKIE

JPM DAVPS 4-14
HEE-HEE,
SNORT

WAH-HA-HA!

OKAY! OKAY!
I'M AWAKE!
© 1984 United Feature Syndicate, Inc.

I LOVE IT WHEN THE GOOD HUMOR MAN COMES
DING
DING
JIM DAVIS
1-16

I LOVE IT WHEN I GET A POPSICLE

I HATE IT WHEN MY LIPS STICK TO THE ☆@ϟ! POPSICLE

EVER NOTICE HOW MOTHS CIRCLE THE LIGHT?
JIM DAVIS
1-17

LIKE PLANETS ORBITING A DISTANT SUN

I LOVE IT WHEN I GET PHILOSOPHICAL
© 1984 United Feature Syndicate, Inc.

I WONDER WHAT HAPPENS WHEN A MOTH GETS TOO CLOSE TO THE LIGHT
JIM DAVIS
1-18

AYIEEEE!
FOOM!

AT LEAST HE DIDN'T SUFFER

RISE AND SHINE, GARFIELD. IT'S A BRIGHT NEW DAY!
1-2-84
JIM DAVIS

IT'S GONNA BE A WONDERFUL DAY, A GREAT DAY!

I THINK I OVER-CHEERFULED IT

HOW DO YOU WANT YOUR COFFEE, GARFIELD?
MAKE IT SIT UP AND BARK
JIM DAVIS 1-3-84

HOW'S THIS?

JUST RIGHT
© 1983 United Feature Syndicate, Inc.

SHOO!
GARFIELD
JIM DAVIS
3-21

FLIES AND I HAVE A LOT IN COMMON...
GARFIELD

YOU CAN'T KEEP EITHER OF US AWAY FROM FOOD
GARFIELD
© 1984 United Feature Syndicate,Inc.

JIM DAVIS
7-13

WAH-HA HA-HA!
I HATE IT WHEN THEY DO THAT
© 1983 United Feature Syndicate, Inc.

WOW! LOOK AT ALL THIS GOOD FOOD AND NEAT CLOTHING!
2-26

THIS IS GREAT STUFF

STAY OUT OF THE TRASH, GARFIELD
HOW DID YOU KNOW?
JIM DAVIS

WHAT A GLORIOUS MORNING!
2-27

I COULD REALLY ENJOY A MORNING LIKE THIS
© 1984 United Feature Syndicate, Inc.
JIM DAVIS

IF I COULD ONLY GET THIS CATCH OUT OF MY BACK

I GOTTA GET HELP FOR THIS CATCH IN MY BACK
JIM DAVIS
2-28

HEY, GUYS

WHAT WE HAVE HERE IS A FAILURE TO COMMUNICATE

MAYBE A GOOD NIGHT'S SLEEP WILL HELP ME GET RID OF THIS CATCH IN MY BACK
JIM DAVIS
2-29

MAYBE NOT

I HATE HAVING A CATCH IN MY BACK. I GET NO SLEEP, I GET NO FOOD, I GET NO EXERCISE

© 1984 United Feature Syndicate, Inc.
JIM DAVIS
3-1

DON'T TIP THE CAT OVER, ODIE
I GET NO RESPECT

WELL HELLO THERE, MR. STUCK-UP
JIM DAVIS
3-2

HAVING A CATCH IN ONE'S BACK DOES TEND TO GIVE ONE AN AIR OF SOPHISTICATION...

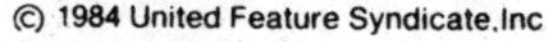

I COULD GET TO LIKE THIS

LET'S TAKE CARE OF THAT CATCH IN YOUR BACK, GARFIELD
JIM DAVIS

CRINK!

3-3

THERE YOU GO, OLD BUDDY
THANKS, I THINK

YOUR BIRTHDAY GIFT IS INSIDE THIS CARD, GARFIELD
JIM DAVIS 6-18

SOMEDAY, MY SIGNATURE WILL BE WORTH A LOT OF MONEY!

© 1983 United Feature Syndicate, Inc.

DON'T WORRY ABOUT YOUR CONDITION, GARFIELD
JIM DAVIS
8-12

YOU CAN STILL LEAD A USEFUL AND PRODUCTIVE LIFE

AS A PAPERWEIGHT, A DOORSTOP, A...
PUT YOUR FACE CLOSER TO THESE CLAWS
© 1983 United Feature Syndicate, Inc.

JIM DAVIS
6-5

SQUIRT

OKAY! WHO GREASED MY WIENER?!
© 1983 United Feature Syndicate, Inc.

GO FETCH THE PAPER, GARFIELD
12-28
JIM DAVIS

LOOK CLOSELY, JON. THESE ARE CAT'S PAWS, NOT SLAVE'S PAWS

I'LL IGNORE YOUR SMALL INDISCRETION THIS TIME, AND SPARE YOUR LIFE
THANK YOU, ... SIR

JIM DAVIS
8-29

THAT WASN'T VERY NICE, GARFIELD
IN THIS BUSINESS, "NICE" DOESN'T PUT BREAD ON THE TABLE
© 1983 United Feature Syndicate, Inc.

JIM DAVIS
1-17

I LOVE IT WHEN THEY ENTERTAIN ME

I'D BETTER SAVE SOME OF THIS BLUEBERRY PIE FOR JON. TO EAT IT ALL WOULD BE INCONSIDERATE AND SELFISH
JIM DAVIS
2-24

I AM WHAT I AM
© 1983 United Feature Syndicate, Inc.

DINNERTIME, GARFIELD!
JIM DAVIS
GARFIELD
3-26

BANZAI
GARFIELD

LD

I CAN'T BELIEVE I TURN SIX YEARS OLD TOMORROW. SOME CATS SAY, "LIFE BEGINS AT SIX," BUT I DON'T BUY THAT
JIM DAVIS
6-18

OLD AGE MAY TAKE ITS TOLL ON SOME CATS, BUT IT'S NOT GOING TO HAPPEN TO ME! I'M GOING TO DO SOMETHING ABOUT IT!

RIGHT AFTER MY NAP

HAPPY BIRTHDAY, GARFIELD! I GOT YOU A RUBBER CHICKEN. THEY'RE LOTS OF FUN!
WE'LL SEE ABOUT THAT
6-19
JIM DAVIS

SMACK
ODIE
SPLUT

CHICKEN, YOU AND I ARE GOING TO HAVE SOME GOOD TIMES

YOU NEED A NAME, FELLA. LET'S SEE... WHAT DO YOU NAME A RUBBER CHICKEN?
6·20
JIM DAVIS

RRRRR

"STRETCH"!
SNAP
© 1984 United Feature Syndicate, Inc.

JIM DAVIS
PECK
PECK
PECK
6-21

SMACK!
© 1984 United Feature Syndicate,Inc

I'LL HAVE SOME HAM AND EGGS, AND MY FRIEND, STRETCH, WILL HAVE A BOWL OF RUBBER BANDS

PECK
PECK
PECK
JIM DAVIS
6-22

STOP PECKING ME WITH THAT RUBBER CHICKEN!

AW, LOOK, YOU HURT STRETCH'S FEELINGS
HE BRINGS OUT THE WORST IN ME

POOKY, I WOULD LIKE YOU TO MEET STRETCH, MY RUBBER CHICKEN
JIM DAVIS
6-23

QUITE FRANKLY, POOKY AND STRETCH DON'T HAVE A LOT OF PERSONALITY

BUT YOU HAVE TO TRADE OFF SOMETHING WHEN YOU SURROUND YOURSELF WITH GOOD LISTENERS

THEY SAY THE FIRST THING TO GO ON A CAT IS ITS HEARING
JIM DAVIS
6-17

OR WAS THAT EYESIGHT?
© 1983 United Feature Syndicate, Inc.

GARFIELD, IF YOU MESS WITH MY NEW FISH, YOU'LL REGRET IT
7-20
JIM DAVIS

WHAT'S SO REGRETTABLE ABOUT A LITTLE SEAFOOD SNACK?

JON'S GOING TO PAY FOR THIS

JIM DAVIS 7-21

WELL, WELL, ODIE. I SEE YOU DERIVE GREAT PLEASURE FROM OTHERS' MISFORTUNE
© 1984 United Feature Syndicate, Inc.

SO DO I!
SNAP!

OKAY, YOU TURKEYS, I'M PREPARED FOR ANYTHING
JIM DAVIS
7-19

♪AROOOO♫

CRASH!

GARFIELD, DID YOU EAT MY FERN?
© 1982 United Feature Syndicate, Inc.

WHY IS IT I GET BLAMED FOR EVERYTHING AROUND HERE? IF SOMETHING GOES WRONG, YOU JUST LAY IT ON OL' GARFIELD!
12-11
JIM DAVIS

I HAVE NO IDEA WHAT YOU'RE TALKING ABOUT

Garfield
Here's Looking At You

JIM DAVIS

RR

OH, GARFIELD
JIM DAVIS

WHAT HAPPENED TO MY CANDY CARAMELS?
11-11

MON'T MOOK AT MEEF
© 1981 United Feature Syndicate, Inc.

OBOY! PIZZA!
JIM DAVIS
11-6

UH-OH

OKAY, WHO'S IN THERE?
AIN'T NOBODY HERE BUT US ANCHOVIES
© 1981 United Feature Syndicate, Inc.

WHY DON'T WE RUN OUT THERE AND EAT ALL THE FOOD?
MY OWNER WON'T LET US
10-17
JIM DAVIS

THEN LET'S KILL HIM

IT IS NOT WISE TO RUB OUT THE HAND THAT FEEDS YOU
CAN I NIBBLE THE TOES OUT OF HIS SWEAT SOCKS?
© 1981 United Feature Syndicate, Inc.

OH NO! I FEEL A NAP ATTACK COMING ON. BUT THE MOVIE'S ALMOST OVER. I MUST STAY AWAKE!
1-9
JIM DAVIS

© 1981 United Feature Syndicate, Inc.
Z

DO YOU KNOW WHY I HATE NERMAL?
JIM DAVIS

IT'S NOT BECAUSE HE'S SO YOUNG, TINY AND CUTE...
9-1

HE REMINDS ME I'M SO OLD, FAT AND UGLY
© 1981 United Feature Syndicate, Inc.

WELL IF IT ISN'T NERMAL, THE SHIRLEY TEMPLE OF THE FELINE SET
JIM DAVIS
8-31

HOW'S IT GOING, NERMAL?
OH, ABOUT THE SAME. I'M OVER-ADORED AS USUAL

© 1981 United Feature Syndicate, Inc.

EAT YOUR FOOD, GARFIELD
NO. IT'S YUKKY
JIM DAVIS
2-25

HOW WOULD YOU LIKE TO GO TO BED WITHOUT DINNER?

SOMEHOW, THAT PSYCHOLOGY DOESN'T SEEM TO WORK ON GARFIELD
© 1981 United Feature Syndicate, Inc.

IT'S YAWN AND CRICK TIME
JIM DAVIS
2-24

YAWN

CRICK!
© 1981 United Feature Syndicate, Inc.

BOY, WHAT A GREAT NIGHT'S SLEEP
YAWN
JIM DAVIS
1-10

HEY, GARFIELD. LET'S GO JOGGING

Z

I'M BORED...BORED, BORED, BORED. THINGS COULD BE WORSE I GUESS
9-23
JPM DAVIS

SPLOOT

BINGO

JUST REMEMBER, GARFIELD, WHEN WE GET TO THE FARM YOU ARE THERE TO RELAX
JIM DAVIS
3-30

I KNOW LAST TIME YOU WANTED TO BE HELPFUL...

BUT YOU DO NOT GROW CHICKENS BY PLANTING CHICKENS IN THE GROUND!
IT WAS AN HONEST MISTAKE
© 1981 United Feature Syndicate, Inc.

OUT !
JIM DAVIS
6-2

YOU CAN SCRATCH MY CHAIR, YOU CAN INSULT MY MOTHER, YOU CAN BEAT UP MY DOG, AND YOU CAN PLAY WITH MY RUBBER MOUSIE...

BUT YOU DON'T EAT MY FOOD AND YOU DON'T SLEEP IN MY BED
YES, SIR

COME HERE, NERMAL
6-4

MAKE YOURSELF USEFUL
JIM DAVIS

WHERE ARE YOU GOING?
TROLLING FOR DOGS
© 1981 United Feature Syndicate, Inc.

HEY, GARFIELD. LET'S SPEND TODAY CELEBRATING ALL THAT'S GOOD IN MANKIND
12-7
JIM DAVIS

LET'S DO A GOOD DEED FOR A STRANGER, STOP AND SMELL A FLOWER AND COMPLIMENT A FRIEND

THAT'S A HEAVY THING TO LAY ON A CAT FIRST THING IN THE MORNING
© 1981 United Feature Syndicate, Inc.

WOULD YOU LIKE TO GO CAMPING, GARFIELD?
JIM DAVIS

WHAT?! AND GET WET WHEN IT RAINS, FREEZE AT NIGHT AND GET THORNS IN MY PAWS?!

WE'LL HAVE PAN-BAKED LASAGNA
I'M PACKED. LET'S GO
5-18

EVERYTHING'S PACKED FOR THE CAMPING TRIP, GARFIELD. DID I FORGET ANYTHING?
JIM DAVIS

ANYTHING ELSE?
YES, 250 MILES OF EXTENSION CORD
5-19

JIM DAVIS
5-20

THERE'S ONLY ONE THING I LIKE ABOUT CARS

THE UPHOLSTERED CEILINGS

BOING
BOING
JIM DAVIS
5-22

ARE YOU BORED, GARFIELD?

HE'LL FIND OUT HOW BORED I AM IF I DON'T GET TO A LITTER BOX SOON
© 198 United Feature Syndicate, Inc.

JIM DAVIS
5-21

GARFIELD! GET OUT OF THERE!

THE LIGHT **DOES** TURN OFF WHEN THE GLOVE COMPARTMENT IS CLOSED
© 1981 United Feature Syndicate, Inc.

GET OUT OF THE CAR, GARFIELD
JIM DAVIS

LET US BASK IN THE SUN AND SLEEP WITH NATURE'S CREATURES, GARFIELD
5-23

TRANSLATION: "LET'S BAKE OUR BRAINS AND LIE ON THE GROUND WITH BUGS AND SNAKES, GARFIELD"
© 1981 United Feature Syndicate, Inc.

COME ON ACROSS THE CREEK, GARFIELD
5-25
JIM DAVIS

I DON'T KNOW WHY YOU CATS ARE SO AFRAID OF A LITTLE MUD

YOU WOULD BE TOO IF YOU HAD TO WASH YOURSELF WITH YOUR TONGUE
© 1981 United Feature Syndicate, Inc.

WELCOME TO OUR FIRST NIGHT OF CAMPING, GARFIELD, ENJOY
5-26
JIM DAVIS

ROAR!

YOU ENJOY. I'LL BE WAITING IN THE CAR

LOCK YOUR DOOR, GARFIELD. THIS IS A TOUGH NEIGHBORHOOD
JIM DAVIS
5-27

I KNOW

HOW OFTEN DO YOU SEE KIDS HAVING A FIRE HYDRANT EATING CONTEST?
© 1981 United Feature Syndicate, Inc.

JIM DAVIS

5-28
© 1981 United Feature Syndicate, Inc.

JIM DAVIS

TELL ME THAT'S NOT A TRAFFIC COP'S HAT YOU'RE WEARING, GARFIELD
OKAY, IT'S NOT A TRAFFIC COP'S HAT
5-29
© 1981 United Feature Syndicate, Inc.

I'M BORED. I THINK I'LL STEP OUT FOR SOME FRESH AIR
JIM DAVIS
5-30

GARFIELD! WE ARE GOING OVER 50!

SO I NOTICED

WE CATS NAP ANYWHERE, ANY TIME
JIM DAVIS
1-6

EVERYONE SHOULD BE SO LUCKY

WITH THE POSSIBLE EXCEPTION OF AIRLINE PILOTS
© 1981 United Feature Syndicate, Inc.

I'VE BEEN WATCHING TELEVISION TOO LONG
JIM DAVIS

I'D BETTER TAKE A BREAK

© 1981 United Feature Syndicate, Inc.
1-14

GARFIELD
JIM DAVIS
10-28

ONE STEP CLOSER AND I'LL PUT THAT TONGUE IN A SPLINT
GARFIELD

YOU GOTTA SPEAK THEIR LANGUAGE
GARFIELD
© 1981 United Feature Syndicate, Inc.

MAYBE I COULD BE AS POPULAR AS NERMAL IF I LEARNED TO DANCE
JIM DAVIS

9-3

I THINK I HURT SOMETHING
© 1981 United Feature Syndicate, Inc

MINE!
GARFIELD
JIM DAVIS
9-4

GARFIELD

YOURS
GARFIELD

I FEEL LIKE GETTING INTO A BIG FIGHT TODAY
JIM DAVIS
8-6

NOW I FEEL LIKE HOLING UP SOMEWHERE TO WHIMPER FOR A WHILE
© 1981 United Feature Syndicate, Inc

IT'S JUST MY LUCK TO FALL INTO A HOG WALLER
9-24
JIM DAVIS

NOTHING IS LESS APPEALING THAN A MUDDY CAT
© 1981 United Feature Syndicate, Inc.

HELLO THERE, GOOD LOOKIN'
OH SHUT UP

HOW CAN YOU HOGS STAND TO LIE IN A WALLER ALL DAY?
9-25
JIM DAVIS

THE MUD KEEPS THE FLIES OFF AND KEEPS US COOL

AND IF WE EVER GET OUT, THE MUD DRYS INSTANTLY

IT'S TIME TO GO HOME, GARFIELD. LET ME KNOCK THAT MUD OFF YOU
9-26

© 1981 United Feature Syndicate, Inc.
CRACK!

JIM DAVIS
THANKS... I THINK

HERE IT COMES AGAIN!
JIM DAVIS
1-8

NAP ATTACK!

ZZZZ
© 1981 United Feature Syndicate, Inc.

Z
1-7
JIM DAVIS

Z

WHEN GARFIELD NAPS,
HE NAPS **HARD**
Z
© 1981 United Feature Syndicate, Inc.

JIM DAVIS
9-16
HA HA HA!

WHAT A GREAT PLOT, FINE ACTING, SUPER PHOTOGRAPHY
© 1981 United Feature Syndicate, Inc.

I LOVE COMMERCIALS

BRINNNNG!
JIM DAVIS
2-25

I LOVE TO WAKE UP EARLY

THE EARLIER YOU SET YOUR ALARM, THE LONGER YOU CAN OVERSLEEP
© 1981 United Feature Syndicate, Inc.

SLEEP ON MY TEDDY BEAR. WILL YOU?!
Z
JIM DAVIS
12-3

Z

I WISH I COULD DO THAT
Z
© 1981 United Feature Syndicate, Inc.

9-17
JIM DAVIS

YOU'RE NO LONGER A KITTEN, GARFIELD
© 1981 United Feature Syndicate, Inc.

WHAT'S THIS WELLING UP WITHIN MY SOUL?
3-4
JIM DAVIS

BY GOLLY, IT'S MY PRIMAL URGES

CIVILIZATION AS WE KNOW IT MAY COME TO AN END NOW THAT THE **CLAW** IS HERE!
© 1981 United Feature Syndicate, Inc.

THE CLAW SETS OUT TO WREAK HAVOC
JIM DAVIS
3-7

CRASH
BAM
SMASH
WHAM
© 1981 United Feature Syndicate, Inc.

THE CLAW GETS HIS HAVOC WREAKED BY THE FANG

I THINK YOU'RE EATING TOO MUCH SALT, GARFIELD. I'M GOING TO TAKE IT OUT OF YOUR DIET
JIM DAVIS

IF YOU MUST
© 1981 United Feature Syndicate, Inc.
7-20

BUT I'M SURE GOING TO MISS MY SALT LICK
GARFIELD

CLAWS
3-3
JIM DAVIS

THOCK!

THE ONLY WAY TO EAT OLIVES
© 1981 United Feature Syndicate, Inc.

I'M HUNGRY... NAH, I'M TOO TIRED TO BE HUNGRY... NAH, I'M TOO DEPRESSED TO BE TIRED
JIM DAVIS
8-23

YUP

IT'S MONDAY
© 1982 United Feature Syndicate, Inc.

JIM DAVIS
1-18

GOOD MORNING...

...GARFIELD
CAFFEINE MAKES ME NERVOUS

FOOD, FOOD, FOOD, IS THAT ALL YOU THINK ABOUT, GARFIELD?
THAT'S ABOUT IT
4-14

© 1982 United Feature Syndicate, Inc.
SO WHAT AM I, CHOPPED LIVER?
JIM DAVIS

DON'T FLATTER YOURSELF
HE CERTAINLY KNOWS HOW TO MAKE A GIRL FEEL GOOD

FOLLOW ME, NERMAL. THIS IS HOW YOU CLIMB A TREE
JIM DAVIS

NOW WHAT DO WE DO?
WHAT A SILLY QUESTION
10-20
© 1982 United Feature Syndicate, Inc.

WE SIT HERE UNTIL THE FIRE DEPARTMENT COMES

THIS WEEK I'M GOING TO CHANGE MY WAYS. I'M GOING TO BEGIN BY NO LONGER HATING MONDAYS
JIM DAVIS
9-6

I'M CRAZY ABOUT MONDAYS. I JUST LOVE MONDAYS

NOW I'M ONLY FOND OF MONDAYS

HELLO. WHAT'S THIS?
JIM DAVIS
3·27

DON'T PANIC, GARFIELD. IT'S ONLY A LITTLE RAIN

AAAAAAAAAAAAA
© 1981 United Feature Syndicate, Inc.

JUST WHAT IS A MONDAY?
JIM DAVIS 5-10
GARFIELD

PLIP
GARFIELD

MONDAY IS A DAY DESIGNED TO ADD DEPRESSION TO AN OTHERWISE HAPPY WEEK

I'M NOT LEAVING BED, I'M NOT MOVING A MUSCLE. IF I DON'T BOTHER MONDAY, MAYBE MONDAY WON'T BOTHER ME
JIM DAVIS
10-18

HELLO, I'M NERMAL, THE WORLD'S CUTEST KITTEN, HERE TO VISIT FOR THE WEEK

WELL, MAYBE I WILL DO JUST A TEENSY BIT OF SOBBING
© 1982 United Feature Syndicate, Inc.

HERE'S HOW TO HANDLE A FIERCE ANIMAL
JIM DAVIS
1-6-82

SHOW NO FEAR

AND SHOW NO PAIN
© 1981 United Feature Syndicate, Inc.

WHAT A DISMAL DAY. I THINK I'LL STAY IN BED ALL DAY
JIM DAVIS
3-8

GOOD MORNING, GARFIELD. IT'S A BEAUTIFUL DAY TODAY

WHAT A BEAUTIFUL DAY. I THINK I'LL STAY IN BED ALL DAY
© 1982 United Feature Syndicate, Inc.

JiM DAViS
3-6

(C) 1982 United Feature Syndicate, Inc.

OH, NO!
JIM DAVIS
9-13

I AM DEFINITELY NOT GETTING OUT OF BED TODAY

NOT ON MONDAY THE 13TH

JIM DAVIS

AHCHOO!
© 1982 United Feature Syndicate, Inc.
3-10

GESUNDHEIT
SNIFF

AND NOW, A WORD FROM OUR SPONSOR
JIM DAVIS
3-11

ZOOM

WELCOME BACK

I HATE MONDAY... SOMETHING BAD ALWAYS HAPPENS TO ME ON MONDAY. IT'S JUST A MATTER OF TIME NOW...
JIM DAVIS
8-2

THE SUSPENSE IS KILLING ME

DO IT TO ME NOW, MONDAY! GET IT OVER WITH!

THE MIRROR IS ONE OF CAT'S BEST FRIENDS, NERMAL. YOU CAN PRIMP IN IT, PLAY WITH IT AND ADMIRE YOURSELF IN IT
JIM DAVIS
10-19

I DON'T SEE WHAT'S SO GREAT ABOUT IT

JIM DAVIS

9·17
© 1984 United Feature Syndicate, Inc

IT'S DIET TIME, GARFIELD
I WAS AFRAID OF THAT

JIM DAVIS
RATS, GARFIELD FELL ASLEEP IN THE MIDDLE OF THE FLOOR
9-15

HAVE YOU EVER TRIED TO PICK UP A SLEEPING CAT?
© 1984 United Feature Syndicate, Inc

IT'S IMPOSSIBLE

OH, NO! A FLEA! I'M GETTING YOU A FLEA COLLAR, GARFIELD
LET'S NOT BE TOO HASTY HERE
11-13

LOOK AT THOSE DISTINCTIVE YELLOW AND GREEN MARKINGS THERE
© 1984 United Feature Syndicate, Inc.

THIS FLEA IS A MEMBER OF A RARE SPECIES OF VEGETARIANS
JIM DAVIS

WELL, THERE'S YOUR NEW FLEA COLLAR, GARFIELD
11-14

WAIT A MINUTE, THERE'S A DISCLAIMER ON THIS BOX. "WARNING: WHILE THIS COLLAR WILL REPEL FLEAS... "
© 1984 United Feature Syndicate, Inc.

"IT HAS BEEN KNOWN TO ATTRACT SHARKS"
JIM DAVIS

DON'T TAKE THAT FLEA COLLAR OFF, GARFIELD!
WHO NEEDS IT?

TUNA
11-15
JIM DAVIS

YOU HAVE A PRETTY GRIM FLEA PROBLEM THERE, ODIE

THAT'S NOT A VERY STRONG FLEA COLLAR

JIM DAVIS 11-16

ONE NICE THING ABOUT CONFIDING IN PETS IS THAT THEY ARE NON-JUDG-MENTAL
JIM DAVIS 9-12

GARFIELD, I GOT A SPEEDING TICKET TODAY

THAT WAS A STUPID THING TO DO
SMACK!
© 1984 United Feature Syndicate, Inc

HEE HEE, THERE'S MORE THAN ONE WAY TO SKIN A CAT
NET WT
JIM DAVIS 9-14
© 1984 United Feature Syndicate, Inc.

WHIRRRRR!

HOW PROPHETIC

HOLD IT RIGHT THERE.
I ALWAYS WANT TO REMEMBER YOU LIKE THIS
GARF
JIM DAVIS

AS THE KIND, BENEVOLENT PROVIDER
GARF

TRYING TO POISON ME WITH THAT CAT FOOD!
GARFIELD
9·25

GARFIELD! COME HERE!
JIM DAVIS
11-12

"GARFIELD" THIS, "GARFIELD" THAT. I'M SICK OF MY NAME

HEY, FLEABAG! COME HERE!
THEN AGAIN, "GARFIELD" DOES HAVE A CERTAIN RING TO IT

ARE YOU IN THERE, GARFIELD?
JIM DAVIS
9-6

THERE AIN'T NOBODY HERE BUT US CHICKENS
© 1984 United Feature Syndicate, Inc.

I WILL NOT SPEAK TO YOUR RUBBER CHICKEN!
THINK OF STRETCH AS MY SOCIAL SECRETARY

JIM DAVIS 8-13

WHAP!

SOMETIME, SOMEWHERE, WHEN YOU ARE LEAST EXPECTING IT... MONDAY STRIKES
© 1984 United Feature Syndicate, Inc.

WHAT'S WRONG WITH THIS PICTURE?
JIM DAVIS 8-14
GARFIEL

THERE'S NO FOOD IN YOUR BOWL, GARFIELD
GIVE THE MAN A CIGAR! FILL IT UP, TURKEY
GARFIEL
© 1984 United Feature Syndicate, Inc.

I HATE IT WHEN LOWER LIFE FORMS ARE CONDESCENDING TO ME

I'VE BEEN TAKEN! THERE WAS ONLY ONE KERNEL OF POPCORN IN THIS WHOLE BAG
POP CORN
POP-A-LOT
JIM DAVIS

OH, WELL, ONE'S BETTER THAN NOTHING
POP CORN
POP-A-LOT

POP!
POP-A-LOT
© 1984 United Feature Syndicate, Inc.
8·15

DOC BOY! HOW'S MY FAVORITE LITTLE BROTHER?
JIM DAVIS
11-19

OH, THINGS ARE PRETTY MUCH THE SAME HERE, WILD PARTIES GOOD TIMES, THE USUAL...

UH, YOU SAY YOU'RE COMING TO VISIT?
IT'S PUT UP OR SHUT UP TIME

WHAT AM I GOING TO DO, GARFIELD? MY BROTHER IS COMING TO VISIT FROM THE FARM
JIM DAVIS
11-20

HE THINKS I LIVE LIFE IN THE FAST LANE
"LIFE IN THE PARKING LOT" IS MORE LIKE IT

I DON'T KNOW WHERE HE GOT THE IDEA
IT WAS WHEN YOU TOLD HIM YOU WERE NEGOTIATING MOVIE RIGHTS TO YOUR DIARY
© 1984 United Feature Syndicate, Inc.

THERE'S MY BROTHER NOW
DING DONG
JIM DAVIS 11·21

WELCOME TO THE BIG CITY, DOC BOY! LET THE GOOD TIMES ROLL!
© 1984 United Feature Syndicate, Inc.

ANOTHER SODA POP?
NO. I THINK I'LL HAVE SOME MORE OF THAT FUN-FILLED POPCORN
I'M GOING TO LIKE DOC BOY

I'M SO EMBARRASSED. DOC BOY COMES ALL THE WAY FROM THE FARM JUST TO FIND OUT WHAT A LOSER I AM
THE TRUTH ALWAYS HURTS
11-22

HEY, WHERE ARE ALL THOSE "GOOD TIMES" YOU PROMISED ME?
WHAT WOULD YOU LIKE TO DO?
JIM DAVIS

LET'S GO TO THE AIRPORT AND WATCH THE AIRPLANES LAND
WHATEVER YOU SAY, WILD MAN!
JON JUST GOT OFF THE HOOK
© 1984 United Feature Syndicate, Inc.

OH, BY THE WAY, DOC BOY, I'VE FIXED US UP ON A DOUBLE DATE
HEY, GREAT!
JPM DAVPS 11-23

WHAT'S A DOUBLE DATE?
THAT'S WHEN YOU AND I GO ON A DATE TOGETHER
© 1984 United Feature Syndicate, Inc.

GEE, IT SEEMS LIKE IT WOULD BE MORE FUN IF SOME GIRLS CAME ALONG
THERE'S NO HOPE

DOC BOY! OUR DATES ARE HERE!

EEEEEEK!
© 1984 United Feature Syndicate, Inc.

JIM DAVIS 11-24
CAN WE TALK?
CAN WE LAUGH?

JIM DAVIS 11-26
I WONDER WHO THAT COULD BE, DOC BOY
DING DONG

DAD! MOM! WHAT ARE YOU DOING HERE!?
WE MISSED YOU BOYS, OKAY?
© 1984 United Feature Syndicate,Inc.

A LITTLE PAINT, A FEW CURTAINS, A WOMAN'S TOUCH, THIS COULD BE NICE!
MY DAD, THE SENTIMENTAL FOOL. MY MOM, THE CLICHÉ

YOUR VISIT IS SUCH A SURPRISE, MOM. WHEN'S THE LAST TIME YOU AND DAD WENT OUT?
WE HAVEN'T BEEN OFF THE FARM SINCE '53
I DON'T BELIEVE THAT

GOOD HEAVENS! WHAT'S THIS?
THAT'S AN INDOOR TOILET, DAD

WOO-HA! AIN'T SCIENCE SOMETHIN'?
FLUSH
NOW I BELIEVE IT
JPM DAVIS 11-27

YOU AWAKE, JON?
OF COURSE NOT, DAD! IT'S 5 A.M.! WHAT ARE YOU DOING UP?
CLICK
11-28
© 1984 United Feature Syndicate, Inc

JIM DAVIS
I GOTTA MILK SOMETHING!
I'M LEAVING

YOU FORGOT THIS WHEN YOU LEFT HOME, DOC BOY
THANKS, MOM. I HAVEN'T SLEPT A WINK WITHOUT IT

WHATCHA GOT THERE, DOC BOY?
NOTHING! NOTHING! IT'S NOTHING!
11-29
JIM DAVIS
© 1984 United Feature Syndicate, Inc.

COULD IT BE A SHRED OF YOUR OLD BLANKIE?
CAREFUL WHAT YOU SAY ABOUT BLANKIES, FELLA

JIM DAVIS 11-30
UH, MOM... I WOULDN'T OPEN THAT IF I WERE YOU

EEEK!
© 1984 United Feature Syndicate, Inc.

SOMETHING IN THERE MOVED!
I'M SURE IT WAS JUST AN OPTICAL ILLUSION
GO AHEAD, TELL HER HOW THE LUNCH MEAT HAS EVOLVED INTO AN INTELLIGENT LIFE FORM

SO LONG, SON. WE GOTTA RUN. I MISS MY COWS
GIVE THEM MY BEST

SEE YUH, DOC BOY! THANKS FOR DECORATING MY HOUSE, MOM!
© 1984 United Feature Syndicate, Inc.
JIM DAVIS 12-1

HELLO... UNDECORATORS?
JON IS A MAN OF GOOD UNTASTE

GARFIELD, I'M GOING TO A CARTOONISTS' CONVENTION, AND THE MOTEL WHERE I'M STAYING WON'T ACCEPT PETS
JIM DAVIS
12-3

SORRY, ODIE. YOU CAN'T GO

GARFIELD, YOU ARE A PET
RATS! I KEEP FORGETTING
SNAP!

I'M LEAVING FOR THE CARTOONISTS' CONVENTION NOW, GARFIELD. THERE'S A WEEK'S WORTH OF FOOD FOR YOU
A WEEK'S WORTH, HUH?
GARFIELD
JIM DAVIS
12-4

GARFIELD

IT WAS MORE LIKE 11 SECONDS' WORTH
GARFIELD

I HOPE JON COMES BACK FROM THAT CONVENTION SOON
JIM DAVIS 12-5

I HOPE I CAN SURVIVE THIS WEEK ON MY OWN

CLICK
I HOPE THAT DOOR ISN'T LOCKED

WHAT A TRAGIC SCENARIO... "OWNER LEAVES FOR WEEK... CAT LOCKS SELF OUT OF HOUSE... CAT STARVES ON FRONT PORCH"
12-6

HEY, WAIT A MINUTE! I CONTROL MY DESTINY! I DON'T HAVE TO STARVE ON THE FRONT PORCH!

JIM DAVIS
© 1984 United Feature Syndicate, Inc.

"CAT STARVES IN BUSHES"

AS LONG AS I'M LOCKED OUT OF THE HOUSE, I GUESS I'LL STRIKE OUT IN SEARCH OF FOOD

GEE, THIS NEIGHBORHOOD DOESN'T LOOK FAMILIAR TO ME
© 1984 United Feature Syndicate, Inc.

OH, NO! WHERE AM I?!
JIM DAVIS
12-7

I GOTTA FIGURE A WAY TO MEET SOME CHICKS
JIM DAVIS 12-8

YOU GOT A PROBLEM THERE, GUY?

STRIKING MANLY POSES DOESN'T SEEM TO BE DOING IT

GARFIELD! I'M BACK FROM THE CONVENTION! WHERE ARE YOU, BIG GUY?... GARFIELD?!
12-10

OH, NO! THIS IS TERRIBLE! GARFIELD DIDN'T GET LOCKED OUT OR ANYTHING, DID HE, ODIE?

YUP
JIM DAVIS

HELLO, GARFIELD
DO I KNOW YOU?
© 1984 United Feature Syndicate,Inc.

LET ME GIVE YOU A HINT... SIT UP STRAIGHT. DON'T TALK WITH YOUR MOUTH FULL. WAKE UP, SLEEPYHEAD

12·11
JIM DAVIS
MOM!

IT'S GREAT SEEING YOU AGAIN, MOM
YES, IT'S BEEN A WHILE
12-12
JIM DAVIS

IT SEEMS LIKE ONLY YESTERDAY

THIS WAS YOUR FIRST BED
IT HAS BEEN A WHILE

MOM, I DON'T RECOGNIZE THIS PLACE. I THOUGHT I WAS BORN IN THE KITCHEN OF AN ITALIAN RESTAURANT
IT CLOSED YEARS AGO, DARLING

IT'S ALL GONE! WHERE'S THE PASTA? THE PEOPLE? THE PASTA? THE EXCITEMENT? THE PASTA?
© 1984 United Feature Syndicate, Inc.

YOU ALWAYS DID LOVE TO EAT
SNIFF... OLD HABITS ARE HARD TO BREAK
JIM DAVIS 12-13

FATHER, THIS IS YOUR GRANDSON, GARFIELD. HE WILL BE STAYING WITH US FOR A WHILE
JIM DAVIS
12·14

IF YOU'RE GOING TO STAY HERE, BOY, YOU'RE GOING TO BE A MOUSER LIKE THE REST OF US

SO THIS IS MY GRANDSON AND YOUR SON, HUH?
MAYBE THEY SWITCHED KITTENS IN THE MATERNITY WARD

IF I HAVE TO BE A MOUSER TO STAY HERE, GRANDPA, I'LL DO IT! I HAVE MADE A NAME FOR MYSELF IN THE MOUSING GAME
12-15
© 1984 United Feature Syndicate, Inc.

THEN EAT THAT MOUSE
ARRRGH!!! PLEASE! PLEASE DON'T MAKE ME EAT IT!

I'D RATHER SWALLOW MY PRIDE THAN THAT MOUSE
JIM DAVIS

GEE, I MISS HAVING GARFIELD AROUND. I EVEN MISS THE ABUSE
JIM DAVIS 12·17

RRR!

THANKS, ODIE, BUT IT JUST ISN'T THE SAME

I'D LOVE TO CATCH YOUR MICE, GRANDPA, BUT I HAVEN'T SEEN ANY WORTHY OF MY TIME. GOT ANYTHING BIGGER?
BRING ON THE TRAINING MOUSE!

JIM DAVIS 12·18

ME AND MY BIG MOUTH

I'M SORRY I CAN'T STAY, MOM
IT'S FOR THE BEST, DEAR. YOU'D BETTER HURRY HOME. IT'S ALMOST CHRISTMAS
JIM DAVIS 12-19

CHRISTMAS! I ALMOST FORGOT!

I ALSO FORGOT I'M LOST

WELL, THIS IS JUST GREAT. I'M COLD, I'M HUNGRY, I'M TIRED...
12-20
JIM DAVIS

IT'S SNOWING TO BEAT THE BAND, AND I HAVEN'T THE FOGGIEST IDEA WHERE I AM

WHILE EVERYONE ELSE IS HAVING A WHITE CHRISTMAS, I'M GOING TO HAVE A WHITE LOST

I'M COLD,
I'M HUNGRY
AND I'M TIRED
JIM DAVIS 12-21

THEY SAY, IN CASES LIKE THIS,
YOU SHOULD FIGHT SLEEP

I SAY,
WHY FIGHT AN
OLD FRIEND?
FOOMP

GARFIELD! WAKE UP! YOU'RE NEAR HOME!
JIM DAVIS 12-22

HUH? MOM? WHA...?!

WOW... IT NEVER LOOKED BETTER

WHERE IS IT WRITTEN THAT HUMANS MUST GIVE CATS MILK IN SAUCERS?! WHY NOT IN CUPS OR BOWLS OR PANS?
8·17
JIM DAVIS

SPLASH!

SEE?!
I THINK GARFIELD IS TRYING TO TELL ME SOMETHING

WHAT IS IT, GARFIELD?
JIM DAVIS

PICK ME UP
TOO FAT TO HOP ON THE TABLE, HUH?
8-18

ONE OF THESE DAYS, I'LL LEARN
© 1984 United Feature Syndicate, Inc.

IT'S MONDAY MORNING. A COLD, GRAY, DRIZZLY MONDAY MORNING
9-24
JIM DAVIS

SOME DUDE WITH A TRUMPET IS WAILIN' SOME BLUES ON THE RADIO AND MY BREAKFAST IS COLD
GARFIELD

IT'S ALL SO PERFECTLY DEPRESSING I CAN'T WIPE THIS SMILE OFF MY FACE
GARFIELD
© 1984 United Feature Syndicate, Inc.

MUNCH
SMACK
SLURP
GARFIELD
9-26

UH-OH!
GARFIELD
JIM DAVIS
© 1984 United Feature Syndicate, Inc.

QUICK-
FOOD

ARFIELD
9-27

BARK!
BLUT!
ARFIELD
© 1984 United Feature Syndicate, Inc.

TWENTY YEARS FROM NOW I'M GOING TO LOOK BACK ON THIS AND LAAAAAAUGH
ROWR
FFFFT!!
JIM DAVIS

OH, COME ON, GARFIELD. THE CAT FOOD ISN'T THAT BAD
GARFIELD

THEN LET'S SEE HOW YOU LIKE IT!
GARFIELD
© 1984 United Feature Syndicate, Inc.
JIM DAVIS

MMM GOOD
YOU LIE!
GARFIELD
9·29

THIS FEELS LIKE
A GREAT DAY TO
SPEND IN BED
JIM DAVIS
10-8

HOP UP, GARFIELD. WE'RE
GOING ON A PICNIC!
GIVE THE BUGS
AND SNAKES
MY REGRETS.
I AIN'T
GOING

I'LL GET YOU
FOR THIS,
MONDAY!

WHAT'S THIS?
I PACKED THE MICROWAVE FOR OUR PICNIC
10-9

WELL, I'M LEAVING IT HERE
JIM DAVIS
© 1984 United Feature Syndicate, Inc.

WHA...!
IF THE TELEVISION STAYS, I STAY

WAIT 'TIL YOU TASTE MY CHERRY PIE, GARFIELD. IT'S THE WORLD'S BEST
JIM DAVIS

I AGREE
10-10

22 MILLION ANTS CAN'T ALL BE WRONG

THE PICNIC'S ALL SET, GARFIELD
JIM DAVIS

DID I FORGET ANYTHING?
© 1984 United Feature Syndicate, Inc.

YOU FORGOT THE BRICK FOR THE TABLECLOTH
10-11

THAT PESKY WIND WON'T SPOIL OUR PICNIC NOW, GARFIELD

WHERE'S THE MUSTARD?
© 1984 United Feature Syndicate, Inc.

UNDER THE THIRD ROCK FROM THE LEFT
JIM DAVIS 10-12

WELL, GARFIELD, THE ANTS ATE MY CHERRY PIE. THE WIND BLEW THE FOOD EVERYWHERE
DON'T SAY IT! DON'T SAY IT!

WHAT ELSE COULD POSSIBLY GO WRONG?
© 1984 United Feature Syndicate, Inc.

YOU SAID IT!
JIM DAVIS
10-13

NO! NO! NO! DON'T MAKE ME DO IT!

ARRRGH! SOMEONE HELP ME!
JIM DAVIS 8-6

SOMETIMES IT'S HARD TO FIGHT PRIMAL INSTINCTS
© 1984 United Feature Syndicate, Inc.

HELLO, LUNCH
8-7
JIM DAVIS

© 1984 United Feature Syndicate, Inc.

THOSE BIRD'S NESTS ARE DECEPTIVELY LARGE

WHY DO I DO IT? WHY DO I CLIMB UP TREES WHEN I CAN'T CLIMB DOWN?
JIM DAVIS
8-8

THE NEIGHBORHOOD ALWAYS TURNS OUT TO SEE ME. THEN THE FIRE DEPARTMENT COMES TO GET ME. THEN MY PICTURE ENDS UP IN THE NEWSPAPER

I JUST ANSWERED MY OWN QUESTION

OH GOOD! HERE COMES A FIREMAN TO SAVE ME!
8-9
JIM DAVIS

TERRIFIC. WHY DO I ALWAYS GET THE FAT ONES?

AND THE ONES WHO ARE SENSITIVE ABOUT THEIR WEIGHT?

I'M GETTING SLEEPY
JIM DAVIS
8-10

IF BIRDS CAN SLEEP IN TREES, SO CAN I

Z

OTHER GARFIELD BOOKS AVAILABLE

Pocket Books		**Price**	**ISBN**
Am I Bothered?		£3.99	978-1-84161-286-7
Compute This!		£3.50	978-1-84161-194-5
Don't Ask!		£3.99	978-1-84161-247-8
Feed Me!		£3.99	978-1-84161-242-3
Get Serious		£3.99	978-1-84161-265-2
Gooooooal!		£3.99	978-1-84161-329-1
Gotcha!		£3.50	978-1-84161-226-3
I Am What I Am!		£3.99	978-1-84161-243-0
I Don't Do Perky		£3.99	978-1-84161-195-2
Kowabunga		£3.99	978-1-84161-246-1
Numero Uno		£3.99	978-1-84161-297-3
Pop Star		£3.50	978-1-84161-151-8
S.W.A.L.K.		£3.50	978-1-84161-225-6
Talk to the Paw	NEW	£3.99	978-1-84161-317-8
Time to Delegate		£3.99	978-1-84161-296-6
Wan2tlk?		£3.99	978-1-84161-264-5
What's Not to Like?		£3.99	978-1-84161-285-0
Theme Books			
Creatures Great & Small		£3.99	978-1-85304-998-9
Entertains You		£4.50	978-1-84161-221-8
Pigging Out		£4.50	978-1-85304-893-7
Slam Dunk!		£4.50	978-1-84161-222-5
The Seasons		£3.99	978-1-85304-999-6
2-in-1 Theme Books			
All In Good Taste		£6.99	978-1-84161-209-6
Easy Does It		£6.99	978-1-84161-191-4
Lazy Daze		£6.99	978-1-84161-208-9
Licensed to Thrill		£6.99	978-1-84161-192-1
Out For The Couch		£6.99	978-1-84161-144-0
The Gruesome Twosome		£6.99	978-1-84161-143-3
Classics			
Volume One		£6.99	978-1-85304-970-5
Volume Two		£7.99	978-1-85304-971-2
Volume Four		£6.99	978-1-85304-997-2
Volume Five		£6.99	978-1-84161-022-1
Volume Six		£7.99	978-1-84161-023-8
Volume Seven		£5.99	978-1-84161-088-7
Volume Eight		£7.99	978-1-84161-089-4
Volume Nine		£6.99	978-1-84161-149-5
Volume Ten		£6.99	978-1-84161-150-1
Volume Eleven		£7.99	978-1-84161-175-4
Volume Twelve		£7.99	978-1-84161-176-1
Volume Thirteen		£6.99	978-1-84161-206-5
Volume Fourteen		£6.99	978-1-84161-207-2
Volume Fifteen		£5.99	978-1-84161-232-4
Volume Sixteen		£5.99	978-1-84161-233-1

Classics (cont'd ...)	**Price**	**ISBN**
Volume Seventeen	£7.99	978-1-84161-250-8
Volume Eighteen	£6.99	978-1-84161 251-5
Volume Nineteen	£6.99	978-1-84161-303-1
Volume Twenty	£6.99	978-1-84161 304-8
Gift Books		
30 years - the fun's just begun	£9.99	978-1-84161-307-9
n't Know, Don't Care	£4.99	978-1-84161-279-9
a Grip	£4.99	978-1-84161-282-9
't Do Ordinary	£4.99	978-1-84161-281-2
your Attitude, I have my own	£4.99	978-1-84161-278-2
Books		
-c-caffeine	£2.50	978-1-84161-183-9
-ood 'n' Fitness	£2.50	978-1-84161-145-7
Laughs	£2.50	978-1-84161-146-4
Love 'n' Stuff	£2.50	978-1-84161-147-1
Surf 'n' Sun	£2.50	978-1-84161-186-0
The Office	£2.50	978-1-84161-184-6
Zzzzzz	£2.50	978-1-84161-185-3
Miscellaneous		
Colour Collection Book 3 (Aug 09)	£11.99	978-1-84161-320-8
Colour Collection Book 2	£10.99	978-1-84161-306-2
Colour Collection Book 1	£10.99	978-1-84161-293-5
Treasury 7	£10.99	978-1-84161-248-5
Treasury 6	£10.99	978-1-84161-229-4
Treasury 5	£10.99	978-1-84161-198-3
Treasury 4	£10.99	978-1-84161-180-8
Treasury 3	£9.99	978-1-84161-142-6

All Garfield books are available at your local bookshop or from the publisher at the address below.

Just send your order with your payment and name and address details to:-

Ravette Publishing Ltd
PO Box 876
Horsham
West Sussex RH12 9GH
(tel: 01403 711443 ... email: ingrid@ravettepub.co.uk)

Prices and availability are subject to change without notice.

Please enclose a cheque or postal order made payable to **Ravette Publishing** to the value of the cover price of the book/s and allow the following for UK postage and packing:-

70p for the first book + 40p for each additional book
except Treasuries & Colour Collections... when please add £3.00 per book